AN INTRODUCTION TO THE GOSPELS
AND ACTS

ESSENTIALS OF BIBLICAL STUDIES

Series Editor
Patricia K. Tull, Louisville Presbyterian Theological Seminary

An Introduction to the Gospels and Acts

ALICIA D. MYERS

OXFORD
UNIVERSITY PRESS

OXFORD

UNIVERSITY PRESS

Oxford University Press is a department of the University of Oxford. It furthers
the University's objective of excellence in research, scholarship, and education
by publishing worldwide. Oxford is a registered trade mark of Oxford University
Press in the UK and certain other countries.

Published in the United States of America by Oxford University Press
198 Madison Avenue, New York, NY 10016, United States of America.

© Oxford University Press 2022

CIP data is on file at the Library of Congress

ISBN 978-0-19-092681-6 (pbk.)
ISBN 978-0-19-092680-9 (hbk.)

DOI: 10.1093/oso/9780190926809.001.0001

1 3 5 7 9 8 6 4 2

Paperback printed by LSC Communications, United States of America
Hardback printed by Bridgeport National Bindery, Inc., United States of America

For Keaton and Gavin,
with the hope that these stories
inspire your own lives as well.

CONTENTS

ILLUSTRATIONS

FIGURES

TABLES

ACKNOWLEDGMENTS

I started this book started in the pre-Covid-19 era but finished most of it during the pandemic. I have many people to thank for their patience and help enabling me to complete this book, even while working at home with two young boys in the house. First and foremost, my husband, Scott, who is a true partner in life. His presence taking care of kids and home, as well as helping me design the maps, is active encouragement for me to continue writing even when social pressures would push me to spend time elsewhere. My boys, to whom this book is dedicated, also deserve thanks; they let their mommy write and came into my office to sneak hugs, give words of encouragement, and to retrieve me for dinner. My professional colleagues and friends at Campbell University have continued to support me in this project as well. Marie Berry and others at Wiggins Library secured interlibrary loans and gathered books from shelves; my academic dean, Derek Hogan, shuffled my course load and let me teach a class on the Christian Apocrypha to facilitate this project; and Jennifer Bashaw joined me in evening conversations and virtual cocktail hours to reflect together on these topics and the best ways to present them to students from all different backgrounds. To my students at Campbell University Divinity School, where I have had the pleasure of teaching for the last seven years: thank you all for, in numerous ways, helping me complete this work. I have patterned this book on the course-work created for our NT 1 class, incorporating insights from our conversations together and the thoughtful questions and perspectives you all bring. I hope you can see some of the fruit of our time together in this work. Finally, I wish to thank Patricia Tull and Steve Wiggins, who invited me to participate in this series. Their feedback and timely conversations helped to make this a better book. I am grateful for their trust in giving me the task of introducing the Gospels and Acts.

SERIES INTRODUCTION

The past three decades have seen an explosion of approaches to study of the Bible, as older exegetical methods have been joined by a variety of literary, anthropological, and social models. Interfaith collaboration has helped change the field, and the advent of more cultural diversity among biblical scholars in the West and around the world has broadened our reading and interpretation of the Bible. These changes have also fueled interest in Scripture's past: both the ancient Near Eastern and Mediterranean worlds out of which Scripture came and the millennia of premodern interpretation through which it traveled to our day. The explosion of information and perspectives is so vast that no one textbook can any longer address the many needs of seminaries and colleges where the Bible is studied.

In addition to these developments in the field itself are changes in the students. Traditionally the domain of seminaries, graduate schools, and college and university religion classes, now biblical study also takes place in a host of alternative venues. As lay leadership in local churches develops, nontraditional, weekend, and online preparatory classes have mushroomed. As seminaries in Africa, Asia, and Latin America grow, particular need for inexpensive, easily available materials is clear. As religious controversies over the Bible's origins and norms continue to dominate the airwaves, congregation members and even curious nonreligious folk seek reliable paths into particular topics. And teachers themselves continue to seek guidance in areas of the ever-expanding field of scriptural study with which they may be less than familiar.

A third wave of changes also makes this series timely: shifts in the publishing industry itself. Technologies and knowledge are shifting so rapidly that large books are out of date almost before they are in print. The internet and the growing popularity of e-books call for flexibility and accessibility in marketing and sales. If the days when one expert can sum up the field in a textbook are gone, also gone are the days when large, expensive multiauthored tomes are attractive to students, teachers, and other readers.

During my own years of seminary teaching, I have tried to find just the right book or books for just the right price, at just the right reading level for my students, with just enough information to orient them without drowning them in excess reading. For all the reasons stated above, this search was all too often less than successful. So I was excited to be asked to help Oxford University Press assemble a select crew of leading scholars to create a series that would respond to such classroom challenges. Essentials of Biblical Studies comprises freestanding, relatively brief, accessibly written books that provide orientation to the Bible's contents, its ancient contexts, its interpretive methods and history, and its themes and figures. Rather than a one-size-had-better-fit-all approach, these books may be mixed and matched to suit the objectives of a variety of classroom venues as well as the needs of individuals wishing to find their way into unfamiliar topics.

I am confident that our book authors will join me in returning enthusiastic thanks to the editorial staff at Oxford University Press for their support and guidance, especially Theo Calderara, who shepherded the project in its early days, and Dr. Steve Wiggins, who has been a most wise and steady partner in this work since joining OUP in 2013.

Patricia K. Tull
Series Editor

ABBREVIATIONS

Abbreviations follow the *SBL Handbook of Style*, 2nd ed. (Atlanta: SBL Press, 2014). Works not included in the handbook are abbreviated as follows.

BRS   Biblical Resource Series
BSL   Biblical Studies Library
BW   BibleWorld
CEB   Contemporary English Bible
HCS   Hellenistic Culture and Society
IJL   Interpreting Johannine Literature
NCBC   New Cambridge Bible Commentary
PROG.   *Progymnasmata* (or *Preliminary Exercises*)
RNT   Reading the New Testament
SNTP   Studies on New Testament Personalities

Introduction

Reading the Gospels and Acts in Context

WHEN WE OPEN OUR NEW Testaments, the first five books we read are stories. Although they are not the earliest documents written in the canon (that honor belongs to the Letters of Paul), they are the stories that form the foundation for the writings that follow. We cannot very well read Paul (or read his writings very well) without first having an idea of who the "Jesus" is who inspired his evangelical and pastoral vigor. The first five books of the canon record and retell stories about Jesus, who early followers came to claim was God's Christ and Son (Matt 1:1; Mark 1:1; Luke 1:35), and even God's Word made flesh (John 1:14–18). The person, Jesus of Nazareth, was regarded by his first followers as the unique messenger and agent of God at the turning of the ages; the one God chose and used to deliver the message of the coming Kingdom of God (or Heaven, in Matthew). The four canonical Gospels—Matthew, Mark, Luke, and John—focus their stories on Jesus himself. They offer related, and connected, narratives about Jesus's beginnings, the start of his ministry, the miracles he performed and conflicts he faced (and caused!), as well as his death, and the proclamation of his resurrection. The book of Acts, however, is different because it focuses more on Jesus's followers than on Jesus himself. The second volume from the author traditionally identified as "Luke," the beloved physician of Col 4:4, Acts tells the story of how the message about Jesus as God's Christ and Son spread from Jerusalem to Rome. Although

An Introduction to the Gospels and Acts. Alicia D. Myers, Oxford University Press. © Oxford University Press 2022. DOI: 10.1093/oso/9780190926809.003.0001

Rome was the center of the world from the point of view of the Roman Empire, it forms part of the "end" of the earth from the perspective of Acts.

Together, these five stories are the focus of our study in this book, but they are not the only writings we will discuss. After all, even though these five books made it into what the later Christians called the "New Testament" (NT), there were other stories about Jesus and the apostles who followed him and spread his message.[1] Early disciples, much like later readers, had questions about Jesus that remained unanswered in the canonical Gospels, and they created and passed down stories meant to teach something else about this unique man, his earthly family, and his first disciples: "What was Jesus like as a child?" for example, or "Why was Mary chosen to be his mother?" Inspired by believers recording and retelling stories about Jesus and his followers, other Christians wrote their own versions of events. These stories share additional interpretations of Jesus and the apostles, who spread Jesus's message far beyond the largely east-to-west route preserved in Acts.[2] This book will help you encounter these writings anew, or even for the first time, prioritizing their messages in the first centuries of the early Christian movement as it developed in the Roman Empire, before considering their continued relevance in our world today.

Before jumping into these stories, then, our first tasks are to understand how this book works and to provide some background on *what* exactly the Gospels and Acts are, as literature and as messages about and from early Jesus-followers. In what follows, I will offer a quick overview of my method and several assumptions to keep in mind as you read. I will then discuss three key issues: (1) the definition of "Gospel" versus the "Gospels"; (2) understanding the Gospels and Acts as literature, with some thoughts on historicity; and (3) the relationships between the four canonical Gospels. Finally, I will give you a short synopsis of the book, summarizing the flow of each chapter.

METHODS AND ASSUMPTIONS

When exploring the writings of the New Testament, bound together in contemporary Bibles of all sorts, it can be easy to forget their complex origins. The Gospels and Acts have their beginnings as stories, some told by Jesus and many told about him, collected and preserved by early followers. It is only later that believers crafted what we call "Gospels"; the Gospel of Mark, first, and then Matthew, Luke, and John. The book of Acts is the second volume to the Gospel of Luke, completing Luke's story by moving from the narrative of Jesus's life, death, resurrection, and ascension, to the events *after* the ascension: the story of the early believers who came to call themselves "Christians" (Acts 11:26). A number of scholars have devoted their attention to reconstructing this complicated oral and compositional past. These methods are called "diachronic"; they seek to reconstruct *how* the writings came to be in their present form *through* (*dia*) *time* (*chronic*). While valuable, I will use synchronic methods in this book. This means I will examine the NT writings in the form we have them today without entering detailed conversations of *how* they arrived in their present forms. More specifically, I will focus on the form available in the New Revised Standard Version (NRSV), which is based on the twenty-seventh edition of the Nestle-Aland Greek New Testament.[3] My intention in focusing on the "final form" of these books is not to deny their complex construction, but, rather, to help you encounter these stories as we have them today. As an introductory text, this book seeks to situate you in these writings and their ancient contexts so that you can continue on to more in-depth studies.

The methods I will use include narrative- and audience-critical approaches.[4] What this means is I will examine the Gospels and Acts as stories (narratives) representing various genres from the ancient Roman world. We will spend time examining main characters, plots, and themes in addition to literary features. I will also devote attention to a variety of historical and contextual elements in each chapter, spreading them out over the course of the book, in order to provide a richer understanding of how these stories could have been heard by their initial audiences. Although we cannot entirely reconstruct the ancient contexts from which these writings come, or the exact ways in which they were read and heard in these contexts, we can formulate probable interpretations by learning as much as we can about the ancient Roman world. In this way, we will tune our ears to hear as closely as we can to how ancients heard them, thus enabling us to pick up on imagery, decipher metaphors and symbols, and uncover meanings to which our ears would otherwise be deaf or mishearing.

As a part of my audience-critical approach, I will use a range of other methods in each chapter, some more traditionally historical-critical in nature, while others are more contemporary, such as disability studies and gender analysis. I will explore one contextual theme per chapter, using the selected theme as a lens for interpreting the biblical book discussed. Beginning with the earliest Gospel, Mark, we will examine the political realities of Roman Palestine that contribute to the apocalyptic outlook of this story of Jesus. Far from a neutral recounting of Jesus's story, Mark's depiction highlights the overlaps between politics and religion that were pervasive in the Roman Empire. In the chapter on Matthew, we will turn our attention to this Gospel's extensive use of Scripture (what Christians now call the "Old Testament")[5] in its portrayal of Jesus as the Messiah. Matthew's quotations of Scripture form only one part of this Gospel's engagement with first-century Judaism, helping us to understand better the complex world in which Jesus lived and of which his first followers were a part.

Reading Luke's Gospel brings us close to a number of people often left on the margins of society, making it a perfect pairing for exploring ancient Roman understandings of identity and humanness. In this chapter, we will ask how class, gender, physical ability, and so on impact one's perceived value in the Roman world *and* in God's Kingdom. The book of Acts continues Luke's story, and his characteristic emphasis on God's inclusiveness, but it also places a special emphasis on the role of the Holy Spirit. This chapter, therefore, will build on previous observations from Luke's Gospel and add to them an examination of conversion, repentance, and the role of spirits in the Roman world. Our study of the Gospel of John will benefit from all the previous chapters while examining in more detail its associations with ancient philosophies and its troubling presentation of the Jews. The final thematic chapter of the book then follows with an examination of additional gospels and acts that did not make it into the NT canon. Found in the so-called Christian Apocrypha, these writings represent some of the most popular extracanonical works of the early Christian movement. Including them in this book not only exposes us to additional interpretations of Jesus and his followers from the ancient world, but also helps us better understand the process of canonization that eventually led to the collection we now call the "New Testament."

The purpose of the narrative and contextual readings presented in this book is not to leave these writings in the ancient world. Instead, these contexts and analyses should enable you to interpret them better in contemporary contexts, as well as see their diverse and ambiguous histories of interpretation. The Gospels and Acts preserved in the Christian NT are stories about Jesus and his first followers, but they are also stories that are intended to shape their audiences, regardless of the century in which they live. The characters in these stories, whether positive, negative, or ambivalent, are portrayed to impact the characters of their audiences. We are made better readers, and shaped to have better characters, when we first seek to understand these writings in their own, ancient contexts. With this foundation, we are prepared to have responsible and ethical interpretations today. Deciphering real connections to the past, as well as real differences, enables us to hear the stories more fully, ask questions even when they make us uncomfortable, and continue encountering the relevance of these writings, even after two thousand years of use, misuse, and even abuse in Western culture.

THE "GOSPEL" AND THE "GOSPELS"

The canonical Gospels have a complicated past. Although this complication includes composition, it begins with their definition as "gospels." Contemporary readers of the four Gospels often assume that a "gospel" is a type of writing, a genre in which the story of Jesus's life, death, and resurrection is told. Yet, while this description does become part of the definition of "gospel" in later centuries, the word's origins actually reach back much farther. When the NT authors (whether they be individuals or groups) responsible for the Gospels and Acts use the word "gospel," it is in connection with the earlier meanings.

The word "gospel" comes from the Greek term *euangelion*, which can also be translated as "good news." This second translation is more transparent to the Greek, which literally means "good" (*eu-*) "message" or "news" (*angelion*). In Greek and Roman contexts, "good news" usually pertained to military conquests and battles. After a victory was secured, a messenger was sent with "good news" to tell the inhabitants of a commander's or king's victory.[6] Messengers were encouraged to bring good news quickly and the first to arrive was welcomed with a reward (*Od.* 14.152–66; Aristophanes, *Eq.* 647; *Plut.* 765). Those who tarried, in contrast, could be punished (Plutarch, *Demetr.* 17.1–5)! When the messenger arrived, the declaration of good news was only the first part of a celebration in the city; it was followed by sacrifices offered to the gods who enabled the victory to be secured as well as the communal consumption of those offerings (Xenophon, *Hell.* 4.3.14; Isocrates, *Areop.* 7.10; Plutarch, *Sert.* 11.1–4). As Gerhard Friedrich explains, the declaration of authentic "good news does not merely declare salvation; it *effects* it."[7] The arrival of the news sparks a celebration as the people begin to live out the salvation effected in the present, as well as looking toward the future. Having been "saved" from ongoing war, salvation means they can appreciate the lives and livelihoods they now have without fear of their imminent destruction.

Similar uses of *euangelion* and its related words are found in the Greek translation of the Old Testament (OT) or Hebrew Bible (HB), which is called the Septuagint (LXX). Although the singular *euangelion* is not found in the LXX, its plural form is, as are various verbal forms (*euangelizō, euangelizomai*). Especially important is the use of these terms in the book of Isaiah. In Isa 40:9–10 the "one delivering good news" (*ho euanglizomenos*) is encouraged to hurry to Zion and tell the troubled city, "See, your God! See, the Lord comes with strength and his arm with authority; see, his reward is with him, and his work before him. He will tend his flock like a shepherd and gather lambs with his arm and comfort those that are with young."[8] This message of comfort and deliverance greets Zion in Isaiah 40–66, sometimes also called Second and Third Isaiah, which describe Judah's return from the Babylonian exile (see also Isa 52:7, 60:6, 61:1). The NT Gospels regularly appeal to this section of Isaiah as a means of describing the arrival of Jesus as God's "Christ" (or Messiah),[9] another term with a connection to Isaiah (Isa 45:1).

Beyond just the LXX, however, other Jewish works make use of the Greek term *euangelion* to describe the "good news" of God's victory on behalf of God's people, often over and against those who oppose them (and, therefore, oppose God). These writings continue building on the sentiment of Isaiah 40–66, often alluding to these writings directly. In exploring the history of the term, scholars note the significance of Isaianic motifs in the Qumran community, who composed the Dead Sea Scrolls.[10] This sectarian Jewish group secluded themselves in the Judean desert in what they believed was a faithful response to Isaiah's command, "A voice cries out in the wilderness, 'Prepare the way of the Lord, make straight in the desert a highway for our God'" (Isa 40:3). The difference in punctuation in my version from the NRSV is intentional; the Qumranites believed they were to go out "in the wilderness" and "in the desert" prepare for God's divine visitation. From their place in the desert, the Qumranites proclaimed the "good news" of God's victory and repeated Isaiah's specific concern for the poor that Jesus likewise proclaims in Luke 4:18–19 (Isa 61:1).

When the NT Gospels use the term "gospel" (and any semantically related words), therefore, they do so in the midst of this rich context. The word itself is not new. What is new is the application of this word to describe Jesus's conception and birth, his ministry, and the story of his death and resurrection. Mark's use of *euangelion* to describe Jesus's proclamation as he travels throughout Galilee resonates with the broader use of the term in the ancient Roman context, while also giving it a particular spin: this is, as expected, "good news" about a kingdom, but it is the "Kingdom of God" as declared by Jesus of Nazareth (Mark 1:14–15). Moreover, by beginning his Gospel with the line, "The beginning of the good news of Jesus Christ," Mark effectively declares his entire story to be "good news" now delivered to all those who hear his account (Mark 1:1). When Jesus arrives with the announcement of his "good news" in Mark 1:14–15, he is the first messenger, the one encouraged to speak in Isa 40:9 and with "beautiful feet" from Isa 52:7. Jesus announces God's victory and the arrival of God's Kingdom, which brings deliverance from oppression, healing, restoration, and justice for God's people. Mark continues telling this news, but lengthens it to include Jesus's ministerial activities, death, and promised resurrection.

Luke, in particular, builds on Mark's use of the Isaianic imagery. In fact, in Luke Jesus quotes from a combination of Isaiah 52 and 61 to describe his arrival and work at his hometown synagogue in Nazareth (Luke 4:16–19; see also Matt 11:5). Jesus will "bring good news to the poor, . . . proclaim release to the captives and recovery of sight to the blind, to let the oppressed go free" (4:18–19). He paraphrases and enacts this mission statement again in Luke 7:20–22 in an attempt to clarify his identity as the Christ to John the Baptist and his confused disciples. After Jesus's death and victorious resurrection, however, the "good news" proclaimed changes. Thus, in the book of Acts, it is no longer just about God's coming Kingdom shared by the chosen messenger, Jesus, but also the news that "Jesus is the Christ" now spread by means of his Spirit-anointed followers (Acts 1:8, 5:42, 8:4–40, 17:18).

The word "gospel," therefore, perhaps imitates Jesus's own use, but it is assuredly grounded in Isaiah's promises and proclamation.[11] The orality of "gospel" is crucial to our understanding of this term. A "gospel" is an active message, brought to a people, and meant to inspire celebration and allegiance. It is not, first and foremost, a book, let alone a fully developed literary genre. In these stories, Jesus speaks the "gospel" of God's coming, and already present, Kingdom. His followers come to understand this message to also include the "good news" of Jesus's death and resurrection in their own evangelizing efforts in Acts, efforts that Jesus first proclaims to them in Acts 1:8. These believers are Jesus's witnesses by continuing to proclaim good news. It is only much later, then, that gospels become recognized as written works. If we fail to note that this is a process, and one that continues even after the first Gospel was written, we will lose sight of the dynamism of Jesus's message, characterization, and reception by his earliest followers.

THE GOSPELS AND ACTS AS LITERATURE

Even though there was a progression from Christians proclaiming a "gospel" to writing "Gospels," that does not mean the NT Gospels themselves have no connections to ancient literature. Instead, when the NT Gospels were collected, written, and edited, they were in the midst of a world accustomed to various techniques and expectations from other types of literature in the ancient Roman world. As part of the extreme minority of people who could read and write, these authors (along with any other people in their communities who actually wrote, composed, collected, edited, and preserved these writings) were educated, at least to some extent.[12] This means they would have been exposed to various genres of literature, performance, argumentation, and rhetorical techniques from the Roman world as well as from Scripture, to which each of the Gospels refers throughout. Although we might often overlook it, the Gospels, like the rest of the NT writings, were composed in a context that prized education and communication, at least for the elite.[13] Education was social capital that showcased status as well as values. When the Gospel authors and other believers take the time to collect, organize, and compose their stories about Jesus, they do so in ways that both resonate with their ancient contexts and highlight their own values in contrast to those of the dominant culture.

The Gospels mirror most closely the genre of ancient biography (*bios*), which was a historical type of narrative writing meant to capture and convey the character (*ēthos*) of its subject.[14] This is in contrast to strictly historiographical writings that were to focus more on major events (i.e., wars) than on the people who participated in them.[15] Biographies record major events and sayings from a subject's life as determined by the author. Authors, of course, were selective about what they included, some offering more details than others. Rather than simple accounts of fact, biographies were written in order to persuade audiences. In particular, they were meant to shape the *characters* (*ēthoi*) of their audiences. Biographies are inherently "ethical" literature, intending to encourage imitation of qualities presented as virtues and avoidance of those presented as vices. In his introduction to his *Life of Aemilius Paullus*, for example, Plutarch explains his goals are to shape his own life after models of virtue, as well as the lives of his audiences (*Aem.* 1.1–8). Philo, too, suggests that his *Life of Moses* should encourage his readers to imitate Moses's virtue (1.155–62). Like these other ancient biographies, the canonical Gospels retell Jesus's life story by exploring recognizable commonplaces (*topoi*) assumed to be indicative of a person's character. These topoi include "origin, nature, training, disposition, age, fortune, morality, action, speech, manner of death, and what followed death."[16] Rather than always retelling these events in chronological order, however, ancients could organize material by theme or topos, such as describing all the public shows a subject sponsored in his lifetime (Suetonius, *Jul.* 39) or collecting all his parables about seeds in one chapter (Mark 4). They could also combine these approaches, switching between chronological and thematic approaches in a given work.

In these writings, authors had some freedom with their material, so long as it was ultimately deemed clear, concise, and credible.[17] As with contemporary writings, ancients criticized one another's work if it failed to meet accepted standards. What this means for us is that while the four canonical Gospels vary in their telling of Jesus's life story, that does not necessarily mean they were considered poorly written or even unhistorical. Instead, as biographies, the Gospels needed to reflect the accepted Jesus traditions from their own contexts, but they could select from this collection and present them in whatever way was believed most compelling. In other words, communication of truth is more than simply an accurate list of Jesus's itinerary and precise diction. Instead, the goal is to showcase Jesus's entire person, his character, so that it will inspire those who hear the Gospel to imitate his example regardless of the consequences. Such lofty aspirations demand more than a verbatim recording of Jesus's precise movements and speeches; they require interpretation and persuasive power in their communication. Far from lies, our ancient authors and communities would argue this is the *real truth* we should be after. When Luke adds a second volume, a historiography of the movement of the Holy Spirit to spread the gospel to the ends of the earth, he extends this understanding of the truth still further. Having learned that Jesus is God's Christ, Luke argues, one should be compelled to spread this good news to the whole of creation.

THE GOSPELS IN RELATIONSHIP

The discussion in the previous section provides an implied rationale about why there are four Gospels in the NT instead of one. There are four Gospels because we have four different perspectives and interpretations of the Jesus story; and each of them has elements to highlight as true over (and sometimes against) the others. We should not be surprised by this. Different people are bound to remember different events and sayings of Jesus, and they are also bound to interpret even the same things in different ways.[18] That we have four canonical accounts of Jesus's life means we have four differing recollections and renditions of his identity and mission. Rather than a dilution of history, it is an abundance from which to learn about him, as well as about how Jesus was interpreted and reinterpreted by early believers in diverse settings.

In fact, several of the canonical Gospels display awareness of one another, as well as additional Jesus traditions not found elsewhere. Most scholars argue that Mark's account is the oldest, with its brevity, rapid pace, and missing birth and resurrection stories.[19] The authors of Matthew and Luke had access to Mark's account, to which they added their own unique material to fill in some of the gaps, but they also respected Mark's account enough to include large portions of it in their own stories (around 90% of it in Matthew and 50% in Luke). This inclusion is not simply paraphrasing, but verbatim repetition, demonstrating Mark's acceptance among early Christians as containing truthful and compelling depictions of Jesus and his mission. Even if Mark's was not the most beloved Gospel of the early church (Papias, for example, excuses his brevity and missing information),[20] it was accepted and respected; it could not simply be ignored. At least, that's what Matthew and Luke seem to indicate.

In addition to quoting large portions of Mark, Matthew and Luke also repeat material that is only found in their own writings (sometimes called the "double tradition"). A number of scholars argue this indicates the existence of a "sayings source" that they call "Q" or *Quelle* (the German word for "source"). For proponents of the "Two-Source Hypothesis," Matthew and Luke used Mark and Q to write their own Gospels. The problem with this theory, however, is that no manuscripts of Q have ever been found. In recent years, Mark Goodacre has revived the Farrer hypothesis, so named for Austin Farrer, who proposed it in 1955. According to Farrer, there is no Q source. Instead, the order of composition of the Gospels is Mark, then Matthew, and then Luke. Matthew used Mark to write his own version, while Luke used both Mark and Matthew, thus explaining the existence of the "double-tradition" without any need for Q.[21]

The difficulty of all this source work is the inability to prove it with absolute certainty. We do not have any autographs of the Gospels, nor can we access any hypothesized oral and written traditions behind these stories. Indeed, recent scholars have renewed attention to the beginnings of Christian literature, especially the composition of the Gospels. Should Mark's Gospel be seen as a type of rough draft, left purposely unfinished for later authors, such as Matthew and Luke, to complete?[22] Perhaps we have assumed the primacy of orality in unhelpful ways, focusing too much on hypothetical believing communities who collected and eventually knitted together stories to create Gospels for their own, seemingly isolated, use.[23] It might be better to again explore the literary relationships, and perhaps even competition, between the four canonical Gospels as well as their apocryphal partners.[24] Whatever the very beginnings of the written traditions about Jesus, what we now have are four canonical Gospels that show careful literary artistry, even if Mark is notably shorter and missing significant events found in the later Gospels. If it is an incomplete draft, it has a surprisingly complete narrative arch and was preserved rather than tossed aside when "more finished" versions emerged. Moreover, the growing awareness of the literary connections between these writings and those of the Greco-Roman world should caution us against assuming these early Christian authors were simple peasants.[25] The messages of caring for the poor and downtrodden are encased in Gospels that replicate literary forms of the elite, perhaps making their messages all the more countercultural. Rather than asserting one of these more recent theories here, however, I will follow the more established Farrer hypothesis suggested by Goodacre as a sort of middle way in this conversation. I also wish to note the growing trend away from singular communities as the recipients of the individual Gospels. Although I will discuss the Gospel communities, I do not mean to imply that these Gospels were read in isolation or *only* meant for a single group of believers. Instead, the summaries are meant to ground our initial investigation of the Gospels, locating the author in a given context while acknowledging the potential (and, indeed, the reality) of a much wider audience.

The question of where the Gospel of John comes into this discussion is an important one. John's Gospel, unlike the Synoptic tradition of Mark, Matthew, and Luke, does not repeat large swaths of material from these other Gospels. In fact, John often includes material that *no other Gospel has*! If John knew about these other traditions, this Gospel is not beholden to them. The audacity of John's potential ignoring of the Synoptics is part of why Johannine independence was at one time well established among scholars. John must not look like the Synoptics simply because he did not know them. His is the "spiritual gospel" in contrast to their more "historical accounts" (Eusebius, *Hist. eccl.* 6.14.7).

Due to the work of many Johannine scholars, however, the pendulum is now shifting.[26] Indeed, John does seem aware of *some* Synoptic traditions. For example, Jesus clears the temple, albeit at the beginning of his ministry, and states the words with which he is falsely charged in Mark (John 2:19; Mark 15:29); he decries the need to ask God to "save me," which again undercuts Mark's account (John 12:27; Mark 14:30); he includes stories about a Mary and Martha, just like Luke (John 11–12; Luke 10:38–42); and he also has Peter visit Jesus's empty tomb, again like Luke (John 20:5; Luke 24:12). According to Paul Anderson, John reinterprets the Markan tradition *and* could have been among the accounts that influenced Luke's composition.[27] Far from an independent tradition, therefore, John's Gospel participates the larger early Christian reflection and interpretation of the Jesus story, and it should be read as an integral part of the whole rather than an elevated or ahistorical outlier.

MOVING FORWARD

The rest of this book will focus on digging more deeply into the Gospels and Acts individually, while also commenting on their possible relationships to one another as part of the larger collection of early Christian traditions about Jesus and his first disciples. The specific themes I will explore have already been outlined, but I will also follow a pattern within each chapter. Each chapter on the canonized Gospels and Acts contains four parts: (1) "Contextualizing the Composition," which will lay out basic historical background information on each writing as well as explore one especially pertinent historical or cultural issue; (2) "Literary Overview," which will provide a basic outline of the flow and structure of each book, as well as highlight important literary features; (3) "Key Passages and Themes," which will focus on a few selected ideas from each book; and (4) "Conclusions," which draws these lines of interpretation together for reflection. Chapter 7, which focuses on the apocryphal gospels and acts, varies from this format in order to give space to issues of canon formation and adequate summaries of the apocryphal works. It is my hope that this book serves as a solid foundation for your reading of the NT. As a guide, this book is meant to come alongside your reading of the Gospels and Acts, pointing out backgrounds and implications you have not yet seen, or which you have noticed, but perhaps did not have the tools to unpack. I will work through each chapter of material with the assumption that you have read, and are reading, the corresponding material. This book cannot replace your encounters with these texts; it is only meant to provide you a more in-depth and enriched experience as you read and reflect on them yourself.

Mark's Story

The Gospel in Roman Palestine

ALTHOUGH THE GOSPEL OF MARK appears second in the NT canon, it was probably the first of the four to be written and distributed. Matthew and Luke retell significant portions of Mark, and John incorporates Markan elements as well, even if just to undercut them (cf. Mark 14:30 with John 12:27; see introduction). It's better for us to start our study with Mark's version of the "good news" because it is the foundation for later narratives about the life of Jesus of Nazareth, even those outside the NT canon. We will start with the possible context for Mark's composition before moving on to a literary overview, and a section devoted to several important passages and themes.

As you read this chapter, keep your copy of the Gospel of Mark handy. Ideally, you should read it in a way similar to ancient audiences: in one sitting, and without chapter and verse delineations determining your divisions of the story.[1] Keep in mind that ancient audiences would have *heard* the Gospel performed instead of reading it silently on their own. Rather than a dry, sacred text written in columns on vanishingly thin paper, the earliest audiences gathered to watch it read aloud.[2] The Gospel of Mark is not just meant to impact its audiences' beliefs about Jesus, but also to entertain them in the process!

An Introduction to the Gospels and Acts. Alicia D. Myers, Oxford University Press. © Oxford University Press 2022. DOI: 10.1093/oso/9780190926809.003.0002

CONTEXTUALIZING THE COMPOSITION

The Basics: Authorship, Date, and Location

The stories that make up what we now have as the "Gospel according to Mark" probably began as oral traditions, told and retold by witnesses, and later audiences, about the life of a certain Jesus from the small, Galilean village of Nazareth. We have no record of Jesus himself writing down any of his own sayings or deeds; instead, we rely on the stories passed down about him and recorded by his followers. This means we cannot trace the rough drafts of the Gospel of Mark or recover a single "original" version. Rather, the Gospel we have was likely finished around the time of the First Jewish War against Rome (66–73 CE).

The Gospel's traditional location of composition is tied to its attribution. The early church historian Eusebius of Caesarea (ca. 265–339 CE) transmits the tradition that this Gospel was written in Rome by John Mark, the onetime missionary companion of Paul who became a steadfast disciple of Peter. Writing in haste as Peter's execution under Emperor Nero's persecution drew near (64 CE), Mark scrambled to compile what Peter remembered from Jesus's life, death, and promised resurrection.[3] This origin story gives credibility to Mark's account since Peter was the primary spokesperson for the disciples in each canonized Gospel. It also justifies the Gospel's shortcomings. In such circumstances, no one could fault Mark for writing a rushed and incomplete account. It would be the job of later authors to flesh out this initial version.

Recent scholars, though, often question this tale. Rather than necessarily dismissing it as romantic and dramatic fantasy, scholars suggest there are clues in the Gospel itself that point to a different provenance. Mark's Gospel reflects several details from Jerusalem, Palestine, and Syria associated with the events of the First Jewish

War.[4] For example, while in the temple in Mark 11:17, Jesus rebukes the people for making it a "den of robbers." The Greek, however, is better translated as a "rebels' hideout." As the most fortified location in Jerusalem, the temple was used as a fortress for the revolutionaries in 68–70 CE. When the three Roman legions surrounding Jerusalem finally broke into the city after a four-month siege, they looted and destroyed the temple before slaughtering a multitude of remaining inhabitants. Mark's language, then, may reflect Jerusalem's reality during this time period. Additional details, such as Mark's specificity of ethnicity of the "Syrophoenician" woman in 7:26, and the note about Simon of Cyrene's children in 15:21, could also point to a Syrian or Palestinian provenance since such information would be most relevant for someone geographically close enough to the events to know these differences and people.

Regardless of its location of composition, however, scholars agree Mark was written just prior to the destruction of Jerusalem in 70 CE. In Mark 13:14, Jesus warns the disciples (and the audience listening) to flee Jerusalem when they see the "desolating sacrilege standing where it ought not to be." Following this warning is a parenthetical note, "let the reader understand," which instructs the one reading aloud to explain its meaning. Unfortunately, we do not know exactly what that explanation was! Matthew and Luke, both written after the temple's destruction, provide greater clarity. Matthew ties the reference to Daniel, signaling the establishment of an idol at the holy site, but Luke offers us the clearest picture. For Luke, "the desolating sacrilege" is the sight of "Jerusalem surrounded by armies" (21:20), the legions who destroyed, defiled, and plundered the city. Building on Mark's initial version, Matthew and Luke repeat Jesus's instructions for the believers to flee rather than join in the fight (Matt 24:15–22; Luke 21:20–24). While Mark anticipates the temple's demise, Matthew and Luke reflect on the aftermath of this tragedy.

Digging Deeper: Roman Palestine in the First Century

Understanding the political atmosphere of Roman Palestine, as well as the larger Roman Empire, is crucial for interpreting the NT Gospels and Acts. Jesus was a Jewish man living in the Roman Empire, as were his earliest followers. The tension between Rome and the Jewish population of Palestine eventually exploded not only in the First Jewish War, but also a Second (the Bar Kokhba Revolt, 132–36 CE), which was prompted by Emperor Hadrian's actions against the Jews. Traditions describe Hadrian's desire to re-build Jerusalem as a Roman city and a possible prohibition against circumcision. Hadrian renamed Jerusalem Aelia Capitolina, ded-icated it to Jupiter, Rome's patron deity, and planned to establish it as a colony for retired soldiers. When the Jews rebelled for a second time, there was another grueling siege and massacre. From this point on, Hadrian sought to erase Jewish traces in Palestine by changing its name from the "Province of Judea" to "Syria Palestine." He also expelled all Jews from Jerusalem, allowing them to enter only once a year to mourn its destruction and, thus, remember their subjection to Roman power.[5]

Although brutal, this subjugation to Rome in the first and second centuries was only the latest in Judea's series of wars, foreign occupations, and expulsions. Stretching back to the Assyrian (722 BCE) and Babylonian conquests (586 BCE), Jewish occupants of Israel (the "Northern Kingdom") and Judea (the "Southern Kingdom") had been uprooted from their land and dispersed into Gentile lands. It is from this dispersion that we get the term *diaspora*. When the OT narratives pick up the story of some returnees to Judea during the Persian Empire, it only recounts the return of descendants of the Southern Kingdom, who come to the ruins of Jerusalem to rebuild the temple and reestablish themselves in the land (Ezra-Nehemiah). Most Diaspora Jews (or "Judeans"), however, did not return to the land, and the northern tribes were considered completely lost.

The Persians eventually fell to Alexander the Great around 330 BCE. After his sudden death in 322 BCE, the residents of Judea found themselves in a tug of war between two of his successors: the Ptolemies of Egypt and the Seleucids of Syria. The more tolerant Ptolemies were preferred, but eventually lost to the Seleucids. The infamous Seleucid king Antiochus IV Epiphanes enraged the zealous Jews of Judea by outlawing monotheistic worship of YHWH, circumcision, dietary restrictions, and Sabbath observance in order to maintain control of Palestine after an attempted coup. Antiochus's policies sparked the Maccabean Revolt (167–164 BCE), which ousted the Seleucids from Judea and began the brief reign of the Hasmoneans. The story of this war and its aftermath is recorded in 1–4 Maccabees. Lasting only one hundred years, the Hasmoneans were the only Jewish rulers of Judea in this entire span of time. Internal fighting among successors John Hyrcanus II and Aristobulus II, however, led to a call for Roman aid. Rome took the invitation as a means to expand its growing reach (Figure 2.1).

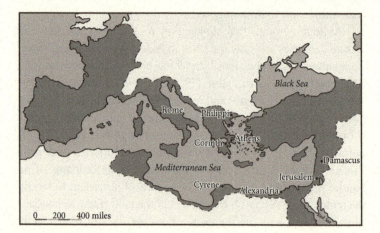

FIGURE 2.1 The Roman Republic in 44 BCE. Rome eventually became an empire when Augustus triumphed at the Battle of Actium in 31 BCE.

Rome sent as its representative Pompey the Great, who not only decided the conflict in favor of Hyrcanus, but also staked the Roman claim on Judea in 63 BCE. To illustrate Roman rule, Pompey marched straight into Jerusalem, into the temple, and all the way into its inner sanctuary, thus declaring all of Judea for Rome. Rome eventually established Herod I (also known as Herod the Great) as a client king, who was tasked with the delicate job of maintaining peace and negotiating Jewish customs with Roman ones. Even though Herod's own paranoid personality, combined with the Judean population's general dislike of him, led to conflict within the royal household (he famously murdered both his wife and son), Herod's reign was largely successful. He built structures throughout Palestine, such as aqueducts that still stand in Caesarea, the fortress of Masada, the Herodium, and Sepphoris, the Roman city where Jesus's father, Joseph, and perhaps Jesus himself practiced their carpentry near Nazareth.

Most importantly, Herod expanded the temple in Jerusalem in an attempt to return it to the grandeur of its Solomonic days. Built with extensive taxes and forced labor, the temple dominated Jerusalem's landscape (see Figure 2.2). Josephus, a Jewish historian from the first century CE, describes the massive building:[6]

> Now the outward face of the temple in its front wanted nothing that was likely to surprise either people's minds or their eyes; for it was covered all over with plates of gold of great weight, and, at the first rising of the sun, reflected back a very fiery splendor, and made those who forced themselves to look upon it to turn their eyes away, just as they would have done at the sun's own rays. But this temple appeared to strangers, when they were coming to it at a distance, like a mountain covered with snow; for as to those parts of it that were not gilt, they were exceeding white. (*J. W.* V.5.6)

The temple was the center of Jewish life in Palestine, as well as of Roman power, since all taxes eventually passed through its walls. It

FIGURE 2.2 Model of the Jerusalem temple, ca. 66 CE. Israel Museum, Jerusalem. The Antonia Fortress, where the Roman soldiers resided and the governor administered when in Jerusalem, is in the upper right-hand corner. Photograph by the author.

is this temple that Jesus enters, teaches in, and disrupts in the NT Gospels.

The Jewish people in Judea (and elsewhere) had to negotiate their faith practices with Roman culture daily. Romans, and Greeks before them, thought Jews were odd for their distinctive practices of male circumcision, food restrictions, and Sabbath observation. Romans generally tolerated Jews due to their antiquity. They did not, however, respect those practices that they considered odd or even barbaric, such as male circumcision.[7] In Judea, Roman authorities routinely experienced tension with Jews, many of whom suffered under Rome's heavy taxation. Rome relied on priests and other Jewish leaders to help keep the peace. Priests of aristocratic class benefited from their roles as moderators and tax administrators, but they also had the precarious job of maintaining equilibrium.

Tensions increased in the lead-up to the First Jewish War over further raises in taxes against the Judean population. When the Roman governor, Gessius Florus, raided the temple to provide for the emperor's treasury and arrested those who resisted, a revolt began in earnest. As was the case with the successful Maccabean Revolt, those fighting saw themselves as God's representatives, ushering in a messianic age of peace and prosperity for the people of Israel. When the rebellion was squashed, the temple was left in ruins, and the priests who had failed to keep the peace no longer had a place to serve. The result was a dramatic reshaping of ancient Jewish practices and self-understanding that we will explore in more detail in the next chapter.

Mark's Cosmic Conflict

The Gospel of Mark was finalized during this time of Jewish conflict with Rome. This knowledge adds vividness to the conflicts Jesus experiences with other authorities in the region. Given the context, it is not surprising that the traditions Mark presents portray Jesus's life as one full of struggle. Jesus encounters resistance from a variety of leaders, both Jewish and Roman, from his own disciples, from would-be followers, as well as from demons and unclean spirits. Far from being welcomed into the cosmos, Jesus faces opposition almost from the outset, even though he brings "good news" that "the Kingdom of God has drawn near" (1:14).

The Gospel argues that, in spite of all appearances to the contrary, Jesus's message was truly one of "good news" even though its proclamation ended with his death by Roman hands. The contrast of the world's appearances with the transcendent truth of heaven is part of Mark's apocalyptic tenor. Even though the word "apocalypse" conjures up images of destruction and death in contemporary Western settings, this word actually means "revelation" or "unveiling." It is also used to describe a worldview that grew out of Persian-era Judaism in response to the extended oppression by foreign rulers. Apocalyptic views eventually developed into a genre of literature, called "apocalypse," that begins in the writings of Isaiah and Daniel, and finds its heyday in the Second Temple period (ca. 515 BCE–70 CE) and continues in Christian writings. New Testament writings convey apocalyptic outlooks that probably trace their roots to Jesus's teachings. Apocalyptic authors and teachers used apocalypticism to explain why things could seem so bad in a cosmos where God remained in control.[8]

Apocalyptic writers operate in binaries. Cosmic, spatial, ethical, and temporal categories are placed in sharp relief: the battle is between God and Satan; God is above all in heaven, and Satan is below on earth; a person is either good or bad; people exist in the present evil age, but look forward to the future, messianic age. Even when the categories blur, they are still decipherable. In Mark, for example, the disciples are ambiguous characters. They sometimes get things right about Jesus, but, more often than not, they get things wrong (e.g., 8:21). Mark's Jesus forgives the disciples when they fail, but he does not praise their confusion. Even with ambiguous characters, the Gospel conveys a basic assumption of good versus evil, better and worse. Like other apocalyptic works, Mark maintains that God has already won the day against the forces of evil.

Mark's unique claim is that God's will is revealed by means of the anointed agent, Jesus of Nazareth, who proclaims the "good news" of God's reign in word, deed, and death. Thus, even though Jesus's death seems to be a defeat, it becomes the climactic evidence of God's in-breaking reign. Indeed, it is just after Jesus dies that the temple curtain is violently ripped from top to bottom, indicating God's breaking out from the heavens and into the world (15:38). This scene connects back to the beginning of the Gospel when the heavens tore, and the spirit descended on Jesus at his baptism while a heavenly voice commissioned him as God's Son and Beloved (1:10). Possessed by God's Spirit, Jesus defeats demonic powers through exorcisms (1:21–28, 5:1–20), performs miracles that subdue the created order (4:35–41, 6:47–51), and bests opponents in verbal feuds (2:1–12, 11:27–12:44). The Gospel claims this is the *real* story of God's work in and though Jesus, but only those who believe in Jesus as the Christ can understand it. Like the disciples in Mark 4:11, the readers have been given the "secret (or mystery) of the Kingdom of God" to see victory where others would only see defeat.

LITERARY OVERVIEW

The Gospel of Mark has a number of characteristic literary features. The Gospel's tempo moves quickly, describing Jesus's travels, miracles, and parables in rapid succession through the first ten chapters. The story then slows down remarkably, saving the final six chapters to describe the last week of Jesus's life, ending with his crucifixion and foretold, but otherwise unseen, resurrection. Later endings were added to the abrupt ending in 16:8; these later witnesses describe Jesus's resurrection in ways that reflect other Gospel traditions, especially Luke and Acts.

Even though the Gospel moves rapidly, it does not rush through events in the narrative. Sayings from Jesus occur in topical collections of parables (4:1–34) and healing stories (1:21–2:12), but the Gospel narrates individual scenes in striking detail. The most apparent of these is the story of John the Baptist's arrest and execution in 6:14–29. Mark's version is longer than both Matthew's (14:1–12) and Luke's (9:7–9). Mark provides more dialogue and vividness to the story, increasing the depth of characterization for Herod and Herodias, as well as Herodias's daughter. Herod, for example, is not just "sorry" for his oaths as in Matt 14:9, but "exceedingly sorry" (Mark 6:26). Mark's brevity and pace should not be mistaken for sloppiness. While not as recognizably rhetorical as Luke, or telling as many stories as Matthew, Mark demonstrates literary finesse that should be appreciated.[9]

Part of this finesse surfaces in the Gospel's frequent use of *inclusios*. This sandwich-type parallelism introduces one idea or story, interrupts its progression with another, before returning to finish the first topic. Mark 5:21–43 offers a classic example of this structure. While traveling to heal Jairus's daughter, Jesus is interrupted by a hemorrhaging woman, who reaches out for healing. Jesus stops to speak to the woman, delaying long enough that Jairus's daughter dies. Jesus, however, resumes his travel with Jairus, encouraging Jairus to trust him along the way. Rebuking the gathered mourners, Jesus ascends the stairs in Jairus's home and raises the girl back to life. The delay invites readers to compare the woman, Jairus, and his daughter, as well as reflect on what they learn from Jesus's behavior. This literary arrangement makes the stories in Mark more memorable and aids in their interpretation since stories are interlaced rather than isolated.

The repetition and many *inclusios* can make the Gospel of Mark difficult to outline in a linear manner. The story looks forward and backward, repeating material and overlapping themes rather than creating distinct divisions in material. The outline below provides a basic overview of the plot:

> The beginning of the good news (1:1–8:30)
>> The beginnings: Jesus's baptism and proclamation (1:1–15)
>> Deeds of power: teaching, healing, and debating near the Sea (1:16–6:6)
>> Food, feasts, and confusion (6:14–8:30)
>
> On the road to Jerusalem (8:31–10:52)
>> Jesus predicts his death (8:31–9:29)
>> Another death prediction (9:30–10:31)
>> The third prediction (10:32–52)
>
> Conflict, death, and promised resurrection (11:1–16:8)
>> Teachings in the temple (11:1–13:37)
>> Last meals and arrest (14:1–52)
>> Interrogations and crucifixion (14:53–15:39)
>> Events after Jesus's death (15:40–16:8)

The beginning of Mark's Gospel offers a synopsis of Jesus's mission after highlighting his anointing by God's Spirit (1:1–15). This beginning also underscores the connection between Jesus's mission and the OT, especially the writings of the prophet Isaiah.[10] Rather than competition between the OT and Jesus's identity and mission, the Gospel of Mark argues they are in full congruence. In fact, Mark presents Jesus's ministry as a sort of "second exodus" event based on the promises from Isaiah of God's restoration of Jerusalem.[11] Even though many may have expected such a restoration to be in the form of a military victory (e.g., like the Maccabean Revolt or hoped for with the First Jewish War), Mark argues that God's victory comes in the guise of a suffering Christ. This surprising revelation may explain why Jesus is so insistent on people keeping his identity a secret until he approaches his death in Jerusalem (cf. 8:31 and 14:62).

The remainder of the first part of the Gospel builds on the introduction with reports of Jesus's deeds and words (1:16–8:30). After his anointing, Jesus demonstrates his connection to God by exorcising demons, healing the sick, calming storms on the sea, and raising a girl from the dead. His actions result in popularity and gossip, but not much understanding. Indeed, the conflicts increase until the midpoint of the Gospel, where Jesus challenges his disciples with the question: "And *you*, who do *you all* say that I am?" (8:29, my translation). Peter responds with the right words: "You are the Christ!" but not with the right meaning (8:30). The second portion of the Gospel records the continued confusion of the disciples, and many others, who cannot comprehend Jesus's predictions of suffering and self-surrender (8:31–10:52).

The third and final portion of the Gospel retells Jesus's last week (11:1–16:8). Arriving in Jerusalem in the lead-up to Passover, Jesus predicts the temple's destruction and earns the ire of those who see him as a threat to Jerusalem's precarious peace. Yet it is Jesus's own disciple, Judas, who ultimately betrays him and the Romans who execute Jesus as a false king. The story ends on the third day after Jesus's death, when the women who had come to anoint his body flee from an empty tomb, unable to tell anyone anything. The Gospel's quick ending leaves the audience with a question: Will the disciples remember Jesus's promise to meet them again in Galilee (14:28, 16:7), or will they remain paralyzed by fear (16:8)?

KEY PASSAGES AND THEMES

Jesus: Possessed and on a Mission

Unlike the other Synoptic Gospels, Mark's story begins with Jesus as an adult. We hear no childhood stories or birth narratives. Instead, the work opens with a declaration:

> The beginning of the good news of Jesus Christ Son of God as it is written in the prophet Isaiah, "See, I am sending my messenger ahead of you, who will prepare your way, the voice of one crying out in the wilderness: Prepare the way of the Lord, make his paths straight." (1:1–3)

The one crying out in the wilderness is John the Baptist, who preaches a "baptism of repentance" so popular it attracts "people from the whole Judean countryside and all the people of Jerusalem" (1:4–5). Not only does John preach repentance, but he proclaims a "stronger one" coming after him who is worthy of greater honor (1:7, my translation). Jesus joins the crowd in 1:9–11, and without any noted interaction, John baptizes him while Jesus experiences a vision: "And just as he was coming up out of the water, *he* saw the heavens torn apart and the Spirit descending like a dove on him. And a voice came from heaven, '*You* are my beloved; with *you* I am well pleased'" (1:10–11). The italicized pronouns highlight the solitary nature of Jesus's vision and auditory oracle. Rather than a statement for all those around him, Jesus's solitary experience sets him apart for the mission that follows in the rest of the Gospel. After being vetted in the wilderness, Jesus returns to declare: "The time is fulfilled, and the kingdom of God has come near: repent and believe in the good news" (1:15).

Without the birth and childhood stories of Matthew and Luke, Mark's Gospel leaves open the possible interpretation that Jesus *becomes* God's Son and Beloved at his baptism. Coming up out of the water, Jesus is anointed and, indeed, possessed by God's Spirit. Even though contemporary contexts refer to "possession" negatively, in the ancient world people believed they could be possessed by a variety of spirits—some good, some bad, and some ambiguous.[12] Whatever "spirit" possessed a person animated that person's behavior and was breathed out in their words. In fact, the word for "breath" and "spirit" is the same in Greek: *pneuma*. In Mark 1:10 the "Spirit descends like a dove *into* him [Jesus]" rather than, as the NRSV translates, "on him." The Spirit does not hover just above Jesus but enters into his body as the source of his works and words in the scenes that follow.

The power of God's Spirit is repeatedly shown in Mark's Gospel. It first drives Jesus out into the wilderness, where he must survive for forty days being "tempted by Satan" (1:12–13). We do not learn any details of this temptation, but from this moment on Jesus is God's representative in Mark's cosmic battle. Possessed by God's Spirit as the chosen Son, Jesus faces off against Satan, the tempter and "ruler of demons" who seeks to destroy God's creation (1:13, 3:22, 5:1–5). During his ministry in Mark, Jesus regularly performs exorcisms. In fact, Jesus's very first action in his public ministry happens in a synagogue in Capernaum where he exorcises an "unclean spirit" from a man (1:21–28). The crowd marvels, "What is this? A new teaching—with authority! He commands even the unclean spirits, and they obey him!" (1:27). Jesus's exorcism of the man is the teaching instead of any words he speaks.[13] Jesus's ability to command the unclean spirit illustrates the victory of God's Spirit over the destructive demonic forces in the world.

Jesus continues his mission as God's agent on earth, facing challenges from demons as well as from people he meets. Unlike most of the people, the demons recognize Jesus as God's Son. They are immediately subdued by him and cannot resist the power of his Spirit-filled words (1:24, 3:11, 5:7, 9:20). Such power instigates fear and suspicion in other powerful figures in the Gospel, such as the religious leaders and Rome-allied authorities. Thus, in Mark 3:22, scribes from Jerusalem conclude: "He [Jesus] has a Beelzebul [a demon], and by the ruler of the demons he casts out demons." Jesus's response is especially sharp, and a bit confusing (3:23–30). He undermines the logic of the experts' opinion ("if a kingdom is divided against itself that kingdom cannot stand," v. 24) and then describes his own works with a metaphor of a thief! Having come to the kingdom, or house, of the "strong one" (i.e., Satan), Jesus is the "stronger one" who binds him in order to "plunder" his house (vv. 25–27). The description of Jesus as the "stronger one" recalls John the Baptist's declaration of the "stronger one" coming after him who will "baptize you with the Holy Spirit" (1:7–8). For Mark's Gospel, Jesus's mission is nothing less than to reclaim God's creation for God alone; this is now the Kingdom, and Household, of God. Jesus ends this episode in Mark 3 by emphasizing that it is not biological or kinship connections that make one part of God's household, or family, but rather obedience: "Whoever does the will of God is my brother and sister and mother!" (3:35).

Jesus's transgressive metaphor in Mark 3 corresponds the transgressive nature of his ministry throughout Mark's Gospel. Jesus regularly confuses and confounds those around him, but he does not give up. As we will see in the next section, Jesus shares the good news, which he allegorizes as "seed" in Mark 4. He sows his message freely, allowing others to react and respond as they will, and perhaps also as God directs. His continued disturbance of the status quo surprises his disciples and infuriates those whose power Jesus threatens, ultimately leading to his crucifixion. But, Mark emphasizes, this too is part of God's plan. Jesus shows God's victory not only in dramatic exorcisms, but also in submission to a gruesome death. Even as Satan's kingdom demonstrates its cruelty in Jesus's crucifixion, Jesus remains "the stronger one" who binds his foe in order to plunder his household. In fact, it is while Jesus hangs on the cross that Rome ironically displays Jesus's kingship with the placard: "King of the Jews" (15:26). And right after his death, a Roman centurion, a representative of Roman power, confesses: "Truly this man was a Son of God!" (15:39).[14]

Mark's Other Characters

In each of the Synoptic Gospels Jesus tells a parable called the "Parable of the Sower" (Mark 4; Matthew 13; Luke 8). This parable is tied to a quotation from Isa 6:9–10 that explains Jesus's rejection by so many who hear him. The reference to Isaiah creates parallelism between Jesus and the well-known prophet of Israel's past. Isaiah was a prophet during the eighth century BCE in Judea, who offered prophetic advice to the kings as recorded in Isaiah 1–39. Isaiah was popular enough to inspire a school of disciples who continued his tradition of teachings long after his death, resulting in the later compilations of Second (Isa 40–55) and Third Isaiah (Isa 56–66). According to his writings, especially Isa 6:9–10, Isaiah prophesied while knowing he would be rejected by the people. Tradition records Isaiah's murder by the wicked king Manasseh, who sawed him in two as he hid inside a tree.[15] Yet some traditions also describe Manasseh's eventual repentance.[16] God's plan was to use Isaiah to warn the people so that, once they experienced judgment, they would return to worship the Lord (Isaiah 40–66). When Jesus quotes Isa 6:9–10, therefore, he recognizes the rejection he will face, but also the larger goal to restore all who listen.

The Parable of the Sower is an allegorical parable because it creates comparisons, or metaphors, that correspond to other realities Jesus explains (4:1–20). In the parable, Jesus describes a "sower," or farmer, casting seed on different types of soil and the results of this free-for-all planting. As in other parables, the image Jesus uses is easily pictured, but it is also shocking. A smart farmer knows the type of soil that will produce the best crop. It is wasteful to throw seed everywhere, but that is exactly what Jesus's "sower" does. The incongruence of the image should grab the attention of Jesus's audience. This is no ordinary farmer, and what he throws is not simply "seed."

The focus turns quickly from the sower to the soils. There are four different types of soil that receive seed: (1) soil "on the path" (or "road") that is quickly eaten by the birds; (2) the "rocky ground" that germinates fast but does not endure extremes; (3) soil already overgrown with thorns that choke out the seed; and finally, (4) the "good soil" that brings forth a record crop (4:4–8). Jesus's allegorical interpretation is given only to "those who were around him along with the twelve" who ask for help understanding his odd farming advice (4:9–20). He reports to them that *he* is the sower, the seed is his *word* (or teaching), and the soils are the *types of people* who hear it. Close readers of Mark find here a basic outline for understanding the characters with whom Jesus interacts throughout the story. It is not that every character *must* cohere to one type of soil, but the allegory clarifies characterizations and contributes to the surprising way Mark elevates otherwise easily overlooked individuals and groups.

The seed thrown on the road, packed tightly from many footsteps and hooves, cannot sink into the ground deeply enough to be protected. The birds swoop in and snatch it away before the seed has a chance to set roots. Jesus explains the birds are like "Satan" who "immediately comes and takes away the word" from those who heard it (4:15). Characters who immediately react negatively to Jesus, without even seeming to contemplate his words, reflect this characterization. Readers often equate the scribes, some Pharisees, and other figures of authority to this group. For Mark, it is not that they are *bad* people; instead, they are victims who have been robbed. Mark assures, however, that Jesus defeats this demonic force in his own temptation (1:12–13) and his plundering Satan's kingdom (3:23–27). These people may not comprehend Jesus's words yet, but that doesn't mean Jesus stops working on their behalf.

The second soil is "rocky." These people receive Jesus's words and excitedly follow, but they don't endure through trials. When we remember that Jesus has a disciple named "Rock" (i.e., Peter), this designation makes sense! Peter quickly follows Jesus and is eager to speak up, please his master, and even *teach him* a thing or two in 8:31! But for all Peter's eagerness, he also represents the disciples with his pervasive misunderstanding of Jesus's mission as God's Christ. Peter cannot understand why Jesus must suffer and, when push comes to shove, Peter abandons Jesus (14:50). He denies Jesus three times at the exact point in time Jesus frankly admits his own identity before the high priest (14:53–72). Peter is a "rocky" Rock, but he too is not without hope. The angel who announces Jesus's resurrection tells the women to testify to Jesus's "disciples *and Peter*" so that they will go and see their risen Lord (16:5–7). Peter may have abandoned Jesus, but Jesus does not abandon him.

The third type of soil is among the thorns. Jesus says these are the people who are surrounded by "the cares of the world, and the lure of wealth, and the desire for other things comes in and choke the word" (4:19). A variety of wealthy and powerful people appear in Mark, such as Herod Antipas, Pontius Pilate, scribes, priests, and other teachers. Not all these people would necessarily be wealthy, but they are in positions of some authority. Any change to the status quo could be a threat, especially in a context rife with tension between Rome in Judea. Those who *are* wealthy, however, regularly respond negatively to Jesus. In 10:17–31, a rich man approaches Jesus asking how he can receive eternal life. The man comes with respect and submits to Jesus, kneeling before him. He knows the Torah well; he can recite to Jesus that he has kept God's commands throughout his life. Yet, when Jesus tells him to sell what he owns and follow him, the man walks away, dejected. This passage demonstrates Mark's view that wealth can be a hindrance (cf. 8:35).

Finally, the fourth type of soil is "good," "noble," or "beautiful" (*kalēn*). This soil produces an abundant crop of "thirty and sixty and a hundredfold" (4:8). In Mark, these are the people who respond to Jesus's words *and* not only hear them but heed them. These are the unnamed individuals and groups who come to Jesus from the margins of society. They pop up in synagogues (1:21–28, 3:1–6), along shorelines and roadsides abandoned by their communities out of fear (5:1–5, 10:46–52), and are children brought by parents for blessings (10:13–16). They are women who charge in and demand healing for a daughter (7:24–31) or who slip in the midst of a crowd to touch the hem of Jesus's garment (5:25–34). Interestingly, these women even surprise Jesus, prompting him to change his own mind about who should benefit from his words or by drawing out power without his consent.[17] Their transgressive behavior shows readers that good soil is not what is considered beautiful by the world. In Mark, it is the world that needs to adjust its definitions!

Jerusalem: Jesus and the Temple

Jesus finally arrives in Jerusalem in Mark 11:1. He enters to great fanfare and a cheering crowd shouting lines from Psalm 118, a song that welcomed the king's arrival.[18] Jesus's entrance not only reminds the audience of ancient Judean kings returning to Jerusalem, but also victorious Roman generals returning to their capital. This sequence is called Jesus's "Triumphal Entry" after the Roman practice of a "triumph," which was a parade where a returning general led his army into the city, displaying the spoils of war. Roman generals rode magnificent chariots flanked by an armed entourage. Dressed in regal purple and crowned with laurel, they were an imposing force that marched through the city to the Temple of Jupiter in the Roman Forum. Once there, the victor offered sacrifices thanking Jupiter for victory. Jewish kings, likewise, came to the temple in Jerusalem to thank the Lord for victory.

In Mark's Gospel, Jesus turns this image on its head. Instead of an imposing force, Jesus enters humbly, on the back of a donkey who has recently given birth. The astounding acquisition of this animal remains known only to the disciples and Gospel audience who hear Jesus give precise predictive instructions to his followers in 11:1–6. The specificity of Jesus's words and their exact fulfillment reinforce the veracity of his death predictions leading up to this moment (8:31–33, 9:31, 10:33–34), as well as his teachings throughout Mark 1–10. The truthfulness of Jesus's words here also alerts the disciples (and the audience) to listen closely as the conflicts, judgments, and predictions continue in Mark 11–14.

Jesus's words in these chapters, however, are not easy to hear. Upon arriving in Jerusalem, Jesus leaves almost immediately. Instead of continuing on to the temple, he turns around and returns to Bethany. He returns the next day, after quizzically condemning a fig tree for having leaves but no fruit; it wasn't even the right time of year for figs (11:12–14)! In the next scene when he enters the temple, he condemns those who turned the temple from a "house of prayer for all the nations" into a "hideout for rebels" (11:17, my translation). This is a judgment against the elite, rather than against everyone who worships in the temple. For Jesus, the temple *looks* like it will be a place of refuge, just as the fig tree with leaves *looks* like it would have fruit. The temple is clearly visible and arresting in its beauty from afar. It attracts people from all around to come and worship. Yet it gives no fruit. It is a home for religious leaders who quarrel with him over scriptural interpretations (11:27–12:44), and even the scribe who Jesus says "is not far from the kingdom" (12:34) remains among many others who desire honor for themselves and take advantage of those they ought to be protecting. Rather than finding life in the temple, the widow puts her "life" (*bios*) in the treasury (12:44–48). While often read as an example of selfless giving, her example is also tragic. The temple and its leaders should protect people like this widow; instead, they are devouring her livelihood and leaving her destitute. The temple, like the fig tree, is condemned, and it too will be destroyed (13:1–2).

The presentation of the temple in Mark is not a condemnation of all things Jewish or the people of Israel. Instead, Jesus's actions parallel those of many Jewish prophets before him. A quick look through Isaiah, Jeremiah, and Ezekiel uncovers harsh words for those in power who use their wealth and influence only to protect themselves instead of protecting the vulnerable: widows, orphans, immigrants, and the poor (e.g., Isa 3:13–15, 10:1–4; Jer 5:20–6:30; Ezekiel 34). Mark's composition during the First Jewish War means the destruction of the temple was looming. Jesus's words give hope to Mark's audiences, showing Jesus knew of this defeat long before it happened. For his disciples, its destruction becomes confirmation that their trust in Jesus as God's Christ is justified.

The fights in and over the temple are ultimately what lead to Jesus's death in the Gospel of Mark. Causing a commotion in the temple would have unsettled the priests responsible for keeping the peace for Rome, particularly before a festival such as Passover. The Antonia Fortress, which housed the Roman forces continually as well as the governor during festivals, towered over the temple, giving the Romans a clear view into the courts they otherwise did not enter. Such a position reasserted Roman control of Jewish worship, as did their control of the high priest's vestments. Jesus's outbursts in the temple could have caught the eye of these watchful overlords, who would have been quick to end any hint of rebellion. Although Mark does not make this fear explicit, as the Gospel of John will, the priests would have sought to prevent an uproar as Passover approached and pilgrims arrived in the city.

Jesus's arrest, interrogations, and eventual trial before Pilate indicate this fear. During his interrogation before the high priest, Jesus is accused of publicly declaring, "I will destroy this sanctuary built by hands and in three days I will build another not built by hands" (14:58, my translation).[19] The destruction of the "sanctuary" (*naon*), the inner part of the temple, would mean not just the destruction of the temple building, but of the entire city and its inhabitants. Jesus is accused of threatening to start a rebellion in the city, one that Pilate and his forces would quell with bloody efficiency. Indeed, that Pilate crucifies Jesus under the inscription "King of the Jews" shows he was concerned that Jesus was a revolutionary. The inscription is an ironic parody meant to humiliate Jesus and scare any other would-be seditionists from acting. *This*, Pilate says, is what rebellion will get you! Bystanders taunt Jesus with the same false accusation in 15:29, therefore showing the correspondence between the Jewish elite and Roman perspectives in Mark.

The climax of all this conflict comes while Jesus hangs on the cross (15:22–42). For the Romans and religious authorities, this seems to be a moment they can relax; they have won the day, the temple is safe, and life will continue without this dangerous, would-be prophet from Galilee. Much in Mark seems to agree with this view. Jesus is abandoned by all his male disciples; only the women look on from afar at his naked, beaten, and suspended form. He is mocked not only by the bystanders on the ground, but also by the two *actual* rebels who hang beside him! Even Jesus's final lament is misunderstood by the spectators. "My God, my God, why have you forsaken me!" (15:34) is heartrending; has Jesus misinterpreted his mission? Jesus's last sounds in Mark are unintelligible, a death cry that mirrors the screams of the exorcised demons from earlier in the Gospel (15:37; cf. 1:26, 5:7). Yet it is at this moment that the earth shakes, the sun hides its light, and the temple (literally, the "sanctuary," *naon*) begins its destruction with the tearing of the veil (15:33–38)! Even a centurion confesses that Jesus is "a Son of God" (15:39). For Mark, Jesus's death is neither easy nor painless, but he faces it willingly in accordance with God's will (14:32–72). God is doing something that will break the world; but a new beginning is not without a painful end, even for God's Beloved (1:9–11).

The End(ings) of Mark

The climactic moment of Jesus's crucifixion quickly descends to a short report of his burial and a shocking scene of women terrified into silence (15:42–16:8). Unlike the other NT Gospels, Mark has no resurrection appearance of Jesus before his disciples. Instead, Mark describes a "young man, dressed in a white robe" reporting this good news to the women at the tomb, instructing them to share it with the disciples and Peter (16:5–7; cf. 14:51–52). For Mark, the disciples need to trust Jesus's words *now* even though they have not lived up to that command in the past. In Mark 14:28, Jesus promised his disciples, "After I am raised up, I will go before you into Galilee." Given the accuracy of Jesus's predictions, especially during his time Jerusalem, the women and men who followed Jesus *should* believe his words and head north. Rather than rejoicing, however, they run away terrified! Instead of reporting the news, Mark ends with the grim words: "And they said nothing to anyone, for they were afraid" (16:8).

While it is surprising for us to end with such a cliffhanger, 16:8 is the place where our oldest manuscripts of the Gospel of Mark do end. Some scholars suggest the real ending of Mark must have been lost. The dissatisfaction with Mark's ending could well be part of what inspired Matthew, Luke, and John to include their much more robust resurrection reports.[20] Later scribes who seem to have known the other Synoptic accounts added longer endings to Mark to clarify things; after all, if the women really hadn't told anyone anything, how was a Gospel written in the first place? These longer endings include a shorter addition in 16:8b, and a longer one in 16:9–20. The connections to Luke and Acts, as well as the distinctive vocabulary of these portions, support the conclusion that they are later additions. The fact that they are additions, however, has not precluded their influence in the Christian tradition. Indeed, snake-handling churches rely on Mark 16:9–20 to support their practices (cf. Acts 28:3–6).[21]

In the Gospel of Mark, we have a clear mixture of traditions and traces of its reception by the early Christians. Ending at 16:8, the Gospel challenges the audience with its incompletion: what will happen next? Remembering that the entire Gospel begins with the phrase "the beginning of the good news of Jesus Christ Son of God" offers one possibility. This story is just the *beginning*; now it is the turn of the audience to decide what they will do with the news they have heard. Will they remain silenced by fear, or will they speak up in faith, regardless of the cost? Some early Christians were not satisfied with this implicit message, and they added explicit answers. Perhaps in a time when the first generation of disciples was dying, or when other Gospels were well known, these Christians wanted to make sure the tradition was recorded in Mark as well. Mark, having achieved a status of authority with

Matthew, Luke, and John, needed to be made more complete. The fluidity of Mark's ending is a good reminder that ancient writings were not as static as we often assume.

CONCLUSIONS

Overall, Mark presents Jesus's life story as a cosmic battle that seeks to right the world's wrongs by elevating the love of God and the love of others. In Jesus's own life, and the life he calls his disciples to imitate, he serves those on the fringes of society and suffers on behalf of others (10:45). Mark's Gospel is fully aware of the difficulty of this calling, and even Jesus struggles with fear of obeying God at all costs (14:36). As God's Spirit-possessed agent, Jesus submits to the divine will and enacts God's apocalyptic, topsy-turvy plan. For Jesus's followers, then, the question Mark continues to ask is whether they will follow Jesus and his model faithfully or succumb to fear.

In contemporary contexts, Mark's message is mixed. It is a good reminder for those in places of power that they should be humble and serve others rather than horde things for themselves. Yet if Mark is used to force ever more sacrifices from those already oppressed by society, its message is unhelpful. After all, Mark does not condemn all kingdoms (or empires), or the hierarchies they assume. Rather, it aims to replace one, Rome's, with another, God's.

When reading Mark and any other Gospel, context remains key. This chapter has emphasized the political and military history of Roman Palestine and the traumas faced by its Jewish inhabitants. In the first century, Jews were a marginalized population even in their Promised Land and holy city. Tension with Roman authorities over taxation and worship practices meant priests and other Jewish leaders had the challenging job of keeping peace without sacrificing faith. The Gospel of Mark, and its main character, Jesus, argue that these attempts have forced leaders to compromise too much with Rome, resulting in oppression of the poor and further exploitation of those who most need protecting. Claiming that God's reign has come in the surprising life, death, and promised resurrection of Jesus, the Gospel of Mark is meant to inspire faithfulness and enduring obedience, even in the face of very legitimate—and very Roman—fears.

Matthew's Story

The Gospel in Jewish Contexts

THE GOSPEL OF MATTHEW WAS probably the second Gospel written even though it is first in the NT canon. Matthew relies heavily on Mark's account, using 90 percent of Mark's material and following Mark's order, but adding significantly to Jesus's lineage, birth, teaching, and resurrection. Matthew shortens several of Mark's more detailed stories, removes some potentially embarrassing ones, and sometimes doubles the numbers Jesus heals (cf. Matt 8:28–33, 9:20–22, 27–31 with Mark 5:1–20, 24–34, 8:22–26). Matthew also has a more intrusive narrator who offers explicit OT quotations to clarify Jesus's teachings and actions. As a result, Matthew's Gospel is, in many ways, more straightforward than Mark's brief, cryptic account. It is unsurprising that Matthew came to be the favorite Gospel of many in the early Christian movement, thus leading to its place at the front of the NT.

This chapter will proceed in the same manner as our last chapter on Mark. I will start with an overview of basic information before delving more deeply into the world behind Matthew. I will then explore the Gospel's literary features and engage with key passages and themes from the book. The Roman imperial context of Judea and Palestine that was the focus of the previous chapter is relevant to Matthew's Gospel as well. This chapter will deepen our understanding by investigating the so-called Jewishness of the Gospel of Matthew in light of first-century Jewish expressions and practices.[1]

An Introduction to the Gospels and Acts. Alicia D. Myers, Oxford University Press. © Oxford University Press 2022. DOI: 10.1093/oso/9780190926809.003.0003

CONTEXTUALIZING THE COMPOSITION

The Basics: Authorship, Date, and Location

Unlike any other canonical Gospel, the traditional author for the "Gospel according to Matthew" is named in this story, even though he is not explicitly identified as its author. The Matthew to whom the writing is attributed is found in 9:9–17. Walking by, Jesus sees a "man called Matthew sitting at the tax booth; and he said to him, 'Follow me.'" Matthew, like the fishermen in 4:18–20 and the scribe in 8:19–20, obediently follows Jesus and even hosts him at his home that evening. Matthew's occupation is clarified in the controversy that follows; he is not just any man at a tax collector's booth, he is a tax collector! He benefited from the Roman imperial systems by collecting taxes on the empire's behalf, as well as taking a share for himself.[2] Matthew was not considered a righteous man when Jesus called on him to be a disciple (9:10–17), but as a disciple, Matthew finds himself included even in the Gospel's prestigious list of the Twelve in 10:1–4 (cf. Mark 3:18).

Although not righteous, Matthew would have been literate, perhaps explaining the early attribution to him. Early Christian traditions from the second century onward all assign a writing to him, often commenting on its composition in Hebrew. Eusebius records Papias's explanation: "Matthew wrote the oracles (*logia*) in the Hebrew language, and everyone interpreted them as he was able" (*Hist. eccl.* 3.39.16). Irenaeus writes, "Matthew also issued a gospel for the Hebrews in their own dialect" (*Haer.* 3.1.1). Yet the Gospel of Matthew shows no signs of having been translated into Greek from Hebrew (or Aramaic), as the LXX does. This association with Hebrew, however, indicates that this Gospel's "Jewishness" was something recognized and perpetuated very early on.

Most contemporary scholars do not think Matthew the tax collector was the author of this Gospel. Instead, some argue the author was a "scribe," partly due to the reference to the "scribe of heaven" in Matt 13:52. This background could explain the extensive use of the OT in Matthew, as well as its common imitation of biblical style. Moreover, Matthew's Gospel does report the inclusion of at least one scribe among Jesus's followers (8:19–20), even if other Jewish religious leaders are portrayed negatively. As with the authorship of the other canonical Gospels, however, recovering the exact author of this work is complicated by the contrast between ancient understandings of authorship and contemporary expectations. Instead of composing the Gospel in its entirety, Matthew could be an authority standing behind these traditions as an eyewitness. Some scholars propose that Matthew's Gospel is the result of a school of disciples who collected, composed, and edited traditions about Jesus for their community's needs.[3] More recently, scholars have pushed against the narrowness of these hypotheses, suggesting a more widespread audience or even a missionary intent for the work (28:19–20).[4] Generally, however, most interpreters emphasize a Jewish-Christian context for the Gospel.

Regardless of the actual author and first audiences of Matthew, this Gospel was composed after the Gospel of Mark; a range between 80 and 100 CE would give the Gospel of Mark time to travel and be interpreted. Many interpreters also advocate an urban setting for Matthew's Gospel that included a mixture of Jews and Gentiles, such as Antioch of Syria.[5] Antioch was an important center for the developing Christian movement and, after the First Jewish War, gained even more significance after Jerusalem's destruction. Like other Roman cities, however, non-Jewish residents of Antioch harbored significant and sometimes violent antagonism for Jews. Riots broke out in the latter half of the first century, during and after the First Jewish War, as Romans reacted negatively to the Jewish revolt.[6] Gentiles called for the revocation of the exemption that allowed Jews to avoid participating in the emperor cult. Instead, Emperor Vespasian taxed the Jews (*fiscus Judaicus*), taking from them the money they would have sent to the temple in Jerusalem to finance a temple to Jupiter in Rome.

The violence faced by Jews, as well as the imposition of a new tax, would have strained the Jewish community in Antioch, particularly if there were a growing group of Jesus-followers in their midst. This might explain some of the anti-Jewish language and characterizations in Matthew. Matthew, like Mark, does not support the First Jewish War, but repeats Jesus's admonitions for believers to flee from Jerusalem when conflict approaches (Matt 24:15–28). Matthew also describes the inclusion of Gentiles with Jesus's Great Commission at the end of the Gospel (28:19). The combination of not supporting the revolt, anti-Jewish biases already present in the Roman world, and the growing number of Gentiles connected to the early Jesus movement contributed to the process we call the "parting of the ways" between Judaism and Christianity. Jesus-followers of Jewish and Gentile descent who did not want (or could not afford) to pay the *fiscus Judaicus* could have pushed this separation further, not knowing the danger it would cause in later years for themselves as well.[7]

Whatever the precise situation that prompted the composition of Matthew's Gospel, the conflict between the Jews who believed Jesus to be the Christ and those who did not is palpable in this story, often resulting in shockingly negative portrayals of Jewish leaders. Matthew's story justifies the Jesus-following Jews (and Gentiles) over and against nonbelieving Jews, highlighting the Jewish nature of Jesus's teaching and ministry even while incorporating language of division and judgment against those who reject him (e.g., 23:1–39, 27:24–25). This context makes the attribution of such a Gospel to a one-time tax collector even more extraordinary in Christian tradition, even if it is ultimately not correct.

Digging Deeper: Jews/Judeans in the First Century

Although we use the term "Jewish" primarily to denote religious expression, ancient Greco-Roman contexts did not have such an understanding. Instead, the word we translate "Jew" simultaneously means "Judean," as in someone either from Judea or descended from Judeans. Along with this ethnic identity were assumed religious practices and beliefs—monotheism, male circumcision, dietary laws, and sabbath observance, to name a few—but there were no credal commitments in the same way that contemporary Christians or Muslims have. In the ancient Mediterranean world, religion was primarily a practice (what one did and did not do) based on your ethnic and social identity. People worshiped whomever and however their father, master, or husband did rather than *choosing* for themselves.[8]

Jewish practices necessarily shifted after the destruction of the First Temple and exile (ca. 587/586 BCE), since the temple (and priests) no longer functioned to enact atonement on behalf of the people. Judeans met, instead, in synagogues as places of prayer, study, and business and family connections. In exile, Judeans faced pressures to conform to the dominant cultures that surrounded them, as the stories of Ezekiel and Daniel illustrate. Even with the return to the land, various groups debated how much Jews could assimilate or resist non-Jewish customs. For Ezra, the separation was absolute: no intermarriage with non-Judeans, and existing ties must be severed (Ezra 10:1–44). For the authors of Second Isaiah, though, God could use even a Persian (and polytheistic) king named Cyrus to bring about deliverance (Isa 44:28). These prior debates over assimilation and resistance offer a helpful lens for understanding the main Jewish groups in the first century CE as well.

Readers of the NT encounter several Jewish groups interacting with Jesus and his followers. Many of these interactions are hostile, establishing the Jewish religious leaders of various stripes as more or less consistent opposition to Jesus's ministry. When we read these exchanges, however, it is crucial that we *contextualize* them, remembering the agendas of our NT authors, their historical situations, and the larger situation of Jews/Judeans in the first century Roman Empire. Instead of thinking of ancient Judaism as a homogenous religion, we should instead think of being Jewish (or Israelite) as being part of a people, whose actual practices and beliefs spanned a spectrum. Debates, sometimes very heated, existed between groups, but they often (though not always) regarded each other as part of the people of God regardless, especially when a common enemy, such as Rome, was involved. Finally, only those who had the leisure to think deeply or participate in systems of power had the time to determine to which smaller group or "school of thought"[9] they belonged. The vast majority of Jews were like the rest of the peasants and poor in the Roman Empire: they were simply trying to get by.

Jewish Schools of Thought in the First Century

Pharisees are probably the best-known Jewish group from the NT, largely because Jesus regularly finds himself in conflict with them in Galilean synagogues. According to Josephus, they were also the most popular group among the people and had some historical alliances with the Herodian family.[10] The Pharisees are the rabbis, or teachers, of ancient synagogues, and they had the responsibility of helping Jews far outside of Jerusalem figure out how to live faithfully in a Gentile world. Although Pharisees supported the temple, they extended holiness to daily practices meant to create a "fence around the law."[11] The fence was made up of "light" laws surrounding the "heavy," or most important laws, such as the Ten Commandments (Exod 20:1–17; Deut 5:6–21). Keeping the lighter laws prevented breaking a weightier one. Yet forgiveness and atonement were available through the temple and individual prayers, like those reflected in the Psalms. Because of their desire to provide guidelines for daily living, the Pharisees collected "traditions of the elders" and considered writings outside of the Torah (Genesis–Deuteronomy) authoritative. Of all the groups, Jesus appears *most* like a Pharisee. This is especially true of the Gospel of Matthew, which also includes scribes among its community (8:19–20, 13:52).

Their creation of writings, as well as their study of Torah, means Pharisees are often connected to *scribes* in the NT. Being a scribe was a profession in both Jewish and non-Jewish communities.

Since most people did not read or write, scribes were specifically trained to use ink, pens (styli), and papyrus to record events, copy manuscripts, take dictation, or even create compositions for clients. In Jewish contexts, scribes are especially associated with the sacred writing that is Scripture. As the recorders and keepers of these writings, scribes knew passages in detail. When Jesus engages a scribe in interpretation, it is with someone who knows Scripture intimately.

Sadducees are another common group in the NT. Connected to the temple in Jerusalem, Sadducees were most often priests from Levitical families, including high priests (Luke 10:32; John 1:19; Acts 4:36). Sadducees competed with the Pharisees for dominance in the Hasmonean period and came to occupy the key negotiating position with Rome because they were the caretakers of the Jerusalem temple. The temple was not only the most important religious site for Jews in the first century, but also a place of significant financial import, collecting taxes and exchanging currency for worshipers and Roman governors alike. For this reason, Josephus presents the Sadducees as the aristocratic class, disliked by the majority of Jews because of their perceived coziness with the Romans.[12]

The Sadducees focused on the Jerusalem temple as the location of God's presence, and on the practice of rituals there to maintain the relationship between the people of Israel and their God.[13] For the Sadducees, God's revelation was offered in the Torah only, which emphasizes the temple cult in connection to Israel's inhabiting the Promised Land. Deuteronomy, in particular, stresses the need to worship in Jerusalem only, as well as insisting both that Israel's eventual expulsion from the land was their fault *and* that God alone is gracious to restore them (Deuteronomy 29–30). From the Sadducees' perspective, God's forgiveness resulted in a return to the land (Ezra–Nehemiah), and they were committed to maintaining the temple to keep this return permanent, even if it meant cooperating with Romans.

Essenes do not appear explicitly in the NT, but Josephus presents them as an ascetic group that separated itself from other Jews in an attempt to keep more strict purity practices. Rather than elitists, Josephus depicts the Essenes as a humble community, whose high standards should be respected. The Essenes were made up of fewer Jews, but they were committed to separating from Roman polytheistic influences.[14] In fact, the community that settled at Qumran near the Dead Sea was probably Essenes who had taken an extreme position against the temple and Sadducees. These Essenes differ from those whom Josephus describes, however, with their polemic against the temple and anticipation of God's imminent eschatological intervention. Some scholars find points of similarity between the apocalyptic views of the NT Gospels and those reflected in several Qumran scrolls, especially *The War Scroll*.[15]

Additional Jewish Groups in the NT Gospels and Acts

Several other groups mentioned in the NT Gospels and Acts are not recognized schools of thought. Members of these groups could also belong to any of the schools above, none at all, or reflect a mixture of perspectives.

Although called the "fourth philosophy" or "school" by Josephus, the *zealots* were not an organized group.[16] Instead, "zeal" has a long history in Judaism, and is often portrayed as a positive trait in OT and Jewish literature (Num 25:11; Ps 69:9; 1 Macc 2:54–58). In general, a zealot could be anyone who was inspired to defend God's honor, even violently. In the first century CE, some specific zealot groups emerged, in addition to the general brigands who roamed the countryside and attacked without clear theological motivation. Josephus describes a group established by Judas the Galilean who declared God alone was King. These zealots promoted the First Jewish War, moving from Galilee south to Jerusalem while attacking Romans, brigands, and other Jews. Another zealot group, the Sicarii ("dagger men"), focused on urban areas, such as Jerusalem, assassinating other Jews who they believed were too closely aligned with Rome. Some suggest it was this group that fled Jerusalem early on in the First Jewish War and met their end with the fall at Masada in 73 CE.

The *Herodians* were aligned with Herod the Great's household (Matt 22:16; Mark 3:6, 12:13). Herod maintained power in Judea from 37 BCE to 4 BCE as the client-king of Rome, and his family had some position of authority in the region until the end of the first century CE. Herod's accommodations to Roman culture were many, including building monuments and cities in honor of emperors. This fact, combined with disputes over his Judean ancestry (his father was an Edomite)[17] and heavy taxation, meant Herod was not a well-loved king. Those who did ally themselves with Herod and his family, however, benefited from that relationship. These Jews were loyal to Herod's successors as well. Figure 3.1 illustrates how Herod the Great's territory was divided among his successors after his death. Herod Antipas ruled over Galilee and Perea (r. 4 BCE–39 CE), while Archelaus ruled Judea, Samaria, and Idumea for only a few years (r. 4 BCE–6 CE). When Archelaus's hold on Judea slipped, Rome sent in a governor (or "procurator") to take his place. Pontius Pilate was assigned to this post from 26 to 36 CE. Herod's other descendants were more successful, including Herod Philip the Tetrarch in Batanea (r. 4 BCE–34 CE), and Herod Agrippa I of Judea (r. 41–44 CE). Herod Agrippa II's reign lasted from around 48 to 93 CE but was disjointed due to the sudden death of his father (Acts 12) as well as the First Jewish War (66–73 CE). It is to Herod Agrippa II that Paul testifies in Acts 26.[18] Keeping the Herods mentioned in the NT sorted is a challenge! Matthew's blending of Herods after his initial description of Herod the Great demonstrates his overall disdain for this dynasty (Matt 2:1–23, 14:1–12).

The *Sanhedrin* was a council of Jewish leaders who had some legal authority prior to 70 CE. There are conflicting accounts of its composition. In the NT, the Sanhedrin is made up of Sadducees and Pharisees, thus leading to Paul's ability to divide them on the

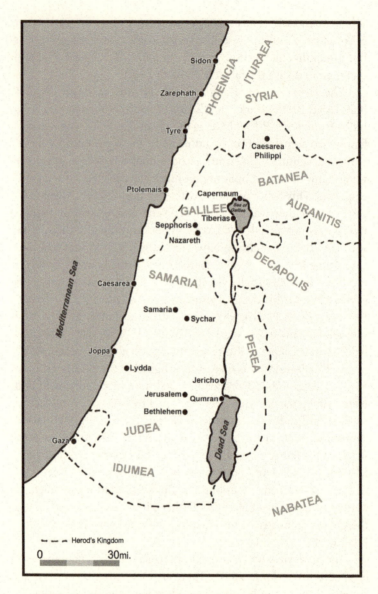

FIGURE 3.1 The Division of Herod the Great's Kingdom.

issue of resurrection in Acts 23:6–10. According to Josephus, however, the Sanhedrin was an impermanent body that formed at the will of the high priest when he deemed it necessary. In rabbinic tradition, the Sanhedrin is composed only of Pharisees, or rabbis, from the time period. Whatever the group's composition, they were subject to Roman oversight even if the Romans gave them some leeway in judicial matters. The diversity of presentations means we should be careful about assuming the depiction of this group in the NT is entirely accurate, particularly since these writings were largely completed *after* the First Jewish War, when the Sanhedrin ceased to exist.

Samaritans were not considered "Judean" or "Jewish" by other Jews in the first century. They were the inhabitants of the land between Judea (southern Palestine) and Galilee (northern Palestine). Although they too worshiped only one God and had a collection of Scriptures similar to the Torah called the "Samaritan Pentateuch," the Samaritans did not recognize the Jerusalem temple as authoritative. Instead, they worshiped at a temple on Mt. Gerizim in Samaria, which was established after the destruction of the first Jerusalem temple by the Babylonians. Samaritans argued that they, unlike the exiled Judeans, maintained the covenant in the land during the exile. According to Jews, however, the Samaritans were not *real* Jews because they married non-Jews during the exile. When the Jews from Babylon returned, they did not acknowledge the Samaritans as legitimate Israelites. This tension led to violent encounters between Jews and Samaritans, especially as Galileans passed through Samaria to travel to and from Jerusalem.

The final group I will mention here is the *Jesus-followers*, the earliest of those who would come to be called "Christians" (Acts 11:26). Jesus and his very first followers, were Jewish. According to the NT, many of them were Galileans, fishermen, tax collectors, and women who supported the group (Luke 8:1–3, 10:34–37; John 11:1–12:8). Others are described as Pharisees even after they became disciples of Jesus and his apostles. Paul is the most famous example, but there is a group of Pharisees mentioned among the believers in Acts 15:5. Even though Christianity is a separate religion today, in the first century and into the beginnings of the second, Jesus-followers were part of the broad spectrum of Jews. This is why questions about dietary laws, sabbath observance, and circumcision were so crucial for the early Jesus movement. Had "Christianity" been separate from the beginning, there would have been no reason for such debates.[19]

The Gospel of Matthew, like the other NT Gospels, should be read as a Jewish writing from the Roman Empire. Matthew is debating how, *not if*, one should follow the God of Israel, by arguing that Jesus is God's chosen Christ. This Gospel is explicit about its connection to Israel's Scriptures, imitating biblical style by beginning with a genealogy (1:1–17) and integrating scriptural quotations, allusions, and references throughout. Often Matthew uses "fulfillment introductions" just before quoting Scripture (1:22, 2:15, 17, 23, 4:14, etc.). In this way, Matthew interprets Jesus's actions as the *continuation* and *fulfillment* of Israel's covenant with YHWH and not as the beginning of a new religion.

LITERARY OVERVIEW

Matthew's literary style differs from Mark's even as it incorporates the majority of Markan material. Matthew often presents events or ideas in threes, a significant number not only in Jewish contexts, but also in rhetorical circles because it added emphasis and aided memory. Matthew reduces the number of *inclusios* from Mark's account, preferring instead to move straight through stories to avoid delays in Jesus's actions or responses to his words (cf. Matt 21:18–19; Mark 11:12–26). Many scholars also note Matthew's rotation between narrative episodes and speeches throughout the Gospel. Read this way, the Gospel divides into six portions of narrative and five speeches:

Narrative 1: Jesus's beginnings (1:1–4:25)
    Speech 1: Sermon on the Mount (5:1–7:29)
Narrative 2: Miraculous works (8:1–9:38)
    Speech 2: Missionary instructions (10:1–11:1)
Narrative 3: Conflict stories (11:2–12:50)
    Speech 3: Teaching in parables (13:1–53)
Narrative 4: Responses to Jesus (13:54–17:27)
    Speech 4: Living in community (18:1–19:1)
Narrative 5: Jesus in Jerusalem (19:2–23:39)
    Speech 5: Looking for the end (24:1–25:46)
Narrative 6: Death, resurrection, and commission (26:1–28:20)

Jesus's five speeches parallel Moses's five books in the Torah (Genesis, Exodus, Leviticus, Numbers, Deuteronomy) as part of a larger comparison between Moses and Jesus in the Gospel. The rotation also highlights Jesus's teachings on various topics as the story progresses. Jesus's discourses often correspond to the events that precede them while setting the stage for what is to come. The Gospel ends with an expanded narrative section describing Jesus's resurrection, the aftermath in Jerusalem, and his commissioning the disciples in Galilee. Unlike Mark, Matthew makes Jesus's resurrection explicit, even providing the story of a cover-up when the Jewish leaders pay off the Roman guards who witnessed it (27:62–28:15). As elsewhere in this Gospel, Matthew brings clarity to what Mark left obscure. Matthew culminates with Jesus's words, spoken again on a mountaintop, encouraging his followers to "go discipling all the nations, baptizing them in the name of the Father, Son, and Holy Spirit" (28:19–20, my translation). With Jesus's ministry complete, the disciples are to carry his message forward.

While the outline above is helpful, it can obscure the plot progression of the Gospel by focusing only on types of prose. A second outline below clarifies the storyline:

Origins and preparation (1:1–4:11)
    Genealogy: Jesus's human lineage (1:1–17)
    Miraculous beginnings: establishing Jesus as God's Son
        (1:18–2:23)
    Transition to adulthood: opposition and God's declara-
        tion (3:1–4:11)

Jesus's ministry as the prophetic Messiah (4:12–20:34)
    John's arrest and the beginning of Jesus's ministry
        (4:12–11:1)
    John's death and reminders of Jesus's beginnings
        (11:2–14:12)
    A good King: Jesus's provision and compassion
        (14:13–16:12)
    Peter's confession and turning toward Jerusalem
        (16:13–20:34)

Fulfillment in Jerusalem and return to Galilee (21:1–28:20)
    Entrance and temple teachings (21:1–25:46)
    Plot enacted: final meals, betrayal, and death (26:1–27:66)
    Resurrection and return to Galilee (28:1–20)

This outline shows that most of Matthew centers on Jesus's teaching, healing, and traveling throughout Galilee. Jesus also prepares his disciples, sending them to teach to "the lost sheep of Israel" (10:5–15) and telling them how to live as a community (18:1–19:1). Rather than focusing mainly on Jesus's passion and death, as Mark does, Matthew highlights the importance of Jesus's life, not only as verifying his identity as God's Christ, but also as containing crucial lessons for followers.

Other significant features in Matthew include the lingering importance of John the Baptist (3:1, 11:11–12, 14:2–8, 16:14, 17:13), God's intervention through dreams of both Jews and Gentiles (1:20, 2:12–13, 19, 22, 27:19), and the use of "Kingdom of Heaven" rather than "Kingdom of God." There is also persistent tension between Jesus and Jewish religious leaders, whom Jesus accuses of hypocrisy (esp. Matthew 23). Alongside these conflicts, Jesus regularly includes judgment scenes in his parables and teachings, describing both eternal life and eternal fire (5:22, 13:40, 42, 50, 18:8–9, 25:41), or "weeping and gnashing of teeth" (8:12, 13:42, 50, 22:13, 24:15, 25:30). According to the Matthean Jesus, daily living should conform to God's will, and everyone will be accountable for their behavior at the Day of Judgment. Although this is difficult for modern readers, it conforms to prophetic teaching, especially in the Book of the Twelve (Hosea–Malachi) and Jewish apocalyptic texts. This aspect of Jesus's teaching is part of the larger interpretation that he fulfills God's promises to Israel. In this Gospel, Jesus is a new Moses, a prophet, and the Son of David. The Gospel urges its audience to take their knowledge of Jesus and his teachings to all the nations, so that many can be blessed by the coming of God's reign (12:18–21, 24:14, 25:42, 28:19).

KEY PASSAGES AND THEMES

Jesus's Origins: Genealogy and Birth (1:1–2:23)

Matthew's Gospel starts with a section most of us probably would just as soon skip: a genealogy. By beginning this way, however, Matthew imitates well-known biblical style from Israel's Scriptures. A quick glance through the books of the OT reveals the common use of genealogies. Matthew begins with the phrase: "A book of the origin (*geneseōs*) of Jesus Christ, Son of David, son of Abraham" (my translation). The word for "origin" can also be translated as "beginning" or "genealogy." It is so common in the book of Genesis that the Greek version of the book was named after it: *genesis*! Matthew uses this word again at 1:18, just after Jesus's genealogy, thereby creating two parallel "beginnings" for Jesus's story: one that starts with his genealogy (1:1–17) and one that records the story of his birth (1:18–23).

Although a bit boring for us—and daunting to read aloud—the first seventeen verses of Matthew's Gospel are carefully arranged: they tie the promises God made to Abraham and David to "Jesus Christ" (Gen 22:15–19; 2 Samuel 7) and form the foundation for Matthew's larger argument that God's promises are fulfilled by Jesus. Matt 1:1–17 falls into three equal subsections corresponding to the titles given to Jesus in 1:1. Verse 17 repeats the genealogy to highlight the important names one more time, while also making sure everyone knows there are fourteen generations between each era. Here's what it looks like:

Introduction: Jesus Christ, Son of David, son of Abraham (v. 1)

    A. From Abraham to David (vv. 2–6a)
    B. From David to Exile (vv. 6b–11)
    C. From Exile to Christ (vv. 12–16)

Summary: fourteen generations each (v. 17)

    A'. Abraham to David (v. 17a)
    B'. David to Exile (v. 17b)
    C'. Exile to Christ (v. 17c)

The results of the careful construction are multiple. First, it emphasizes Jesus's connection to key figures in Israel's past. Certainly, this includes Abraham and David, but also all the people mentioned in each generation. If the audience knew their Jewish history, these names would evoke entire stories and episodes of God's faithfulness. Second, the balance of fourteen generations indicates God's involvement, guiding history to the moment of Jesus's birth as the Christ. Third, the genealogy especially emphasizes royal elements of Jesus's messiahship, since the number fourteen is the sum of the Hebrew letters that spell David's name. The name "David" has three letters in Hebrew: DVD (דוד). When added together, the letters equal fourteen (4 + 6 + 4 = 14).

One more characteristic of Matthew's genealogy must be mentioned: namely, his inclusion of five women. While this seems sparse to us, it is surprising that Matthew included any women at all (cf. Genesis 5, 6, 10, 11, 25, etc.). Moreover, the women included are also surprising: Tamar, Rahab, Ruth, the "wife of Uriah" (aka Bathsheba), and Mary. As many commentators note, all these women have culturally ambiguous sexual experiences.[20] Tamar tricks Judah into having sex with her so she can have children (Genesis 38); Rahab was a prostitute from Jericho (Joshua 2); Ruth was a Moabitess, who were often depicted as sinful seductresses; the "wife of Uriah" was not David's wife, but was raped and her husband murdered by David (2 Sam 11–12); and Mary, whose own conception of Jesus comes into question in Matt 1:18–23. Yet, in spite of these situations, all these women are shown righteous by their actions in contrast to the men who oppress them. Not only do these women reveal how assumptions can be deceiving, but also how, for Matthew, God finds a way to sculpt history despite the failures of those in power: God uses surprising means to upend expectations.

Resuming the "beginning" again, Matt 1:18–23 focuses on Jesus's conception and birth. Although the narrator has clearly identified Jesus in his genealogy, Joseph needs divine intervention to prevent him from divorcing Mary after learning of her untimely pregnancy (1:18–19). With a tactic that repeats at the beginning and end of this Gospel, Matthew describes dreams received first by Joseph (1:20–21), then by the three astrologers ("magi"; 2:12), and Joseph again to secure Jesus's safety during infancy (2:13–23). At the end of the Gospel, Pilate's wife has a divinely given dream, though she and Pilate do not respond rightly to it (27:19). In Matthew 2, Herod is a clear threat to Jesus's life, but Joseph is actually the *first* threat to him: if Mary had been divorced, not only would Jesus's life have been endangered for lack of care, but he would not have been integrated into the Davidic line (1:16).[21] Joseph is assuaged by the "angel of the Lord," who tells him: "Do not be afraid to take Mary as your wife, for the child conceived in her is from the Holy Spirit. She will bear a son and you are to name him Jesus, for he will save his people from their sins" (1:20–21). It is interesting that the "fear" Joseph has is over marriage to Mary rather than of the angel's appearance! Like the other men in Jesus's genealogy, Joseph is in danger of acquiescing to cultural pressures rather than seeing how God works outside of them.

In Matthew, there are three participants in Jesus's conception and birth: a "Holy Spirit" (i.e., God) who begets; Mary, who conceives, gestates, and bears; and Joseph, who names. In spite of her crucial role, Mary is silent throughout Matthew's account and never explicitly *agrees* to be God's chosen vessel. Matthew's focus on Joseph (and other male perspectives) throughout the birth narrative is in keeping with the largely male vantage point of the genealogy. But that vantage point is also undercut by the inclusion of the women mentioned above and whispers of Mary's actions. For Matthew, God is not limited by cultural expectations. Thus, from the outset, Jesus is set up to be a paradoxical figure: he is both the fulfillment of God's long-ordained plan of salvation and also the one who continues God's countercultural methods that bring this plan to completion. At the end of the Gospel, women are again the trusted messengers of God's actions when they obey the risen Jesus's instructions to tell the male disciples of his resurrection (28:1–10).

The Sermon on the Mount (5:1–7:29)

Jesus communicates his paradoxical teaching in speeches throughout the Gospel. As noted above, Jesus gives five speeches in this Gospel, which are collections of sayings rather than actual speeches following rhetorical standards of the day. These collections are arranged topically and, accordingly, can feel fragmented and unfocused to contemporary readers. Slowing down, however, we can see the linking words and themes that flow through these collections and help us have a better understanding of Matthew's interpretation of Jesus's instructions.

Of all the collections of sayings in Matthew, none is as well known as the Sermon on the Mount from Matthew 5–7. This sermon stands out for several reasons: it is both a synopsis of Jesus's teachings and a precursor of future conflicts he will have with religious leaders over scriptural interpretation. It also includes pithy sayings that are memorable outside of their specific context within the sermon. As with the other discourses, Jesus's sayings are put together topically, with the result that Matthew 5–7 resembles works such as Proverbs, James, or other Jewish wisdom literature more than it does a sermon. The following outline highlights the collection's topical flow:

5:1–2. Mountaintop setting
5:3–16. Unusual blessings: the character of disciples
5:17–48. Completion: Jesus's relationship to the Law
6:1–34. Fast, give, and pray with trust rather than fear
7:1–27. Living sincerely: the Golden Rule
7:28–29. Conclusion

The mountaintop setting of 5:1–2 is often compared to Moses's reception of God's revelation on Mt. Sinai (Exodus 19–24). At the beginning of Exodus 19, God promises Israel, saying, "If you obey my voice and keep my covenant, you shall be my treasured possession out of all the peoples. Indeed, the whole earth is mine, but you shall be for me a priestly kingdom and a holy nation" (19:5–6). In many ways, it is at Sinai that Israel is born. Mirroring this moment, Jesus too forms a people for God at the mountain in Matthew 5–7. For Matthew, Jesus is like Moses but greater, since he issues commands from the mountain's peak, the same location where Moses met with the Lord, rather than from the bottom, where Moses teaches (Exod 24:1–2). Jesus's teaching, therefore, seems to come directly from God. Jesus's turn to interpret many of the Mosaic laws (Torah) makes sense in this narrative context. Jesus extends the Torah to become even more strict in order to reinforce its intentions of love and mercy, rather than undercutting them. For Matthew, those who follow Jesus's instructions have an intimate relationship with God, becoming children in God's household. This new household is more important than any human community and is also more trustworthy because God is at its head.

Overall, Jesus's teaching in the Sermon on the Mount emphasizes sincere discipleship that focuses on the "Father in heaven" regardless of the trials, persecutions, temptations, and scarcity oppressing the audience. According to Jesus, this sincerity is the true meaning of the Law and the prophets, another way to refer to Israel's Scriptures (Matt 5:17–20, 7:12). Disciples whose focus is on the heavenly Father will not fear sharing the good news in spite of danger—social or otherwise—and they will not seek rewards from people, but rather live with true faith (5:11–13). Such faith is not just cognitive assent, but results in daily actions, some of which were risky in the first century and today. Jesus gives specific examples to ground his theological and ethical concepts: disciples will not curse others, objectify and use women, seek revenge, or even defend themselves against attack (5:21–42). Instead, like good children, disciples should imitate their Father by loving enemies (5:43–48). So great is a disciple's trust of this Father that everything can be risked for the sake of heavenly rewards.

We should be careful to observe that Jesus's instructions target free men rather than women, children, or slaves. In this way, they parallel much of Jewish literature and Torah interpretations that focus on the obligations of Israelite men rather than everyone attached to them. The assumption is that if the leader of a household lives as Jesus instructs, all those in his care will benefit. The disciples described by Jesus do not take advantage of those in their care or those they could exploit; instead, they focus on what their heavenly Father desires: authentic righteousness exemplified by love and mercy. Thus, the heavenward focus of Jesus's teaching does not result in a detachment from the world, but a readjustment of one's relationship to it. Rather than following human standards and fears of scarcity that lead people to fulfill selfish desires, Jesus's disciples are to trust in their Father's bountiful provision. This does not mean these disciples will never suffer or mourn; Jesus tells them that they will, but that they will be blessed for it. For Matthew, such suffering and mourning will ultimately be balanced with heavenly rewards from their Father, and Jesus himself acts as the primary example for the disciples to follow.

Matthew's Other Characters: A Mixed Reception

The other characters who interact with, or hear about, Jesus in the Gospel of Matthew are challenged by his vision of faithful living. Jesus's teaching is similar in Mark and Luke, but Matthew presents those challenged by Jesus's teachings in a unique way: offering both a more generous presentation of Jesus's disciples and a more polemical one of his opponents, particularly Jewish leaders. This contrast creates a paradox in Matthew: it is considered the most Jewish of the canonical Gospels, but it contains some of the harshest language against the Jews, even statements that have been used by Christians to justify anti-Jewish policies and violence (esp. Matt 27:25).[22] How can this be?

All of Jesus's earliest, and closest, disciples in Matthew are Galilean Jews of various socioeconomic classes. While these people regularly struggle to understand Jesus's actions and words, Matthew presents them as moving from initial confusion to comprehension at key moments in the story. In the last chapter, I used Mark's version of the Parable of the Sower to analyze other characters in that Gospel. Jesus tells this parable in Matthew as well, but instead of reprimanding his disciples for not understanding, Jesus praises the disciples. After quoting Isa 6:9–10, Jesus says: "But blessed are your eyes, for they see, and your ears, for they hear. Truly I tell you, many prophets and righteous people longed to see what you see, but did not see it, and to hear what you hear, but did not hear it"

(Matt 13:16–17). The disciples, then, do not seem to be the same "rocky soil" they were in Mark (cf. Mark 8 with Matthew 16). This presentation perhaps encouraged the Matthean audiences to trust in their leadership, who may have been connected to this first group of disciples. Matthew's message also encourages its audience to trust that despite their own initial misunderstandings, they too would come to understand and be blessed.

In contrast to this generous characterization, Matthew is particularly polemical toward those in power, especially Jewish leaders. Matthew includes stories of Herod the Great's attempts to kill Jesus, and his massacre of infants (2:1–18), as well as the story of Herod Antipas's unjust execution of John the Baptist (14:1–12). Both men occupy thrones as client kings, but neither enacts justice; instead, their fear of losing power leads them to violence, killing rather than protecting those in their care. Jewish religious leaders are likewise characterized negatively in Matthew. While the rare scribe may come to follow Jesus, most leaders are classified as "hypocrites"—the Greek word for an actor, one who pretends to be someone else and hides behind a mask (6:2, 5, 16, 22:18). In Matthew 23 Jesus takes special pains to underscore his distrust of the scribes and Pharisees (23:1–36). Matthew 23–25 includes Jesus's final series of teachings in the temple before his arrest and execution. Here, Jesus foretells judgment against the religious leaders as well as against any who mimic their hypocrisy. In Matthew 26, the plot against Jesus begins, thus implying it was anger over Jesus's words that prompted the "chief priests and the elders of the people" to act (26:1–5; cf. 27:18).

Matthew's language against the Jewish leaders is not only difficult when interpreting the Gospel today, but also when we see it used to justify any anti-Semitism. Many of us easily link these ideas to the horrors of the Holocaust, but anti-Jewish policies and violence were practiced long before then. Western societies have likewise seen recent upticks in anti-Semitism, meaning we need to continue dealing with these troubling texts. Remembering that the Gospel of Matthew is itself a Jewish, rather than a Christian, story is critical in this reflection. Matthew participates in an *internal Jewish debate* over the identity of the Christ, rather than being an outsider's polemic against a different religion. Indeed, as social identity theory demonstrates, people are often (though not always) more critical of those considered part of their group than those who are clearly on the outside.[23] After all, the thought goes, *they should know better*! Indeed, Matthew's polemic against the Jewish leaders regularly has this tone: they know Scripture, so they *should* recognize Jesus as the Christ. Their failure, thus, garners an even sharper rebuke from Matthew's Gospel.

Many scholars seek to tie Matthew's negative characterization of Jewish leaders to the social situation of the Gospel's earliest audiences.[24] Set in a post–70 CE world, these Jesus-followers lived in a time just after the Jerusalem temple's destruction and in the wake of the Roman response to the first Jewish rebellion. From this perspective, many of Jesus's warnings in Matthew 23–25 have already come to fruition. The specific venom Matthew has against Pharisees and scribes might also hint at its post–70 CE reality, since these leaders survived the rebellion, while the Sadducees and other temple authorities did not. The Gospel of Matthew, therefore, is interpreting what it means to be disciples of Jesus after the destruction of the temple, in the midst of a Roman-dominated world, and perhaps at odds with other surviving Jewish groups. The diversity of Jewish expressions outlined above reminds us that such debates were common in the first century, some of them quite heated. Contextualizing Matthew's Gospel in this way does not excuse its language or the anti-Jewish ways it has been and continues to be used, but it does help us understand more clearly *how* Matthew's presentation came about. It should also make us wary of accepting Matthew's presentation wholesale; instead, we should think about what Jesus-followers were facing alongside other Jewish groups in this time period.

CONCLUSIONS

Matthew's Gospel is a story compiled, recorded, composed, and retold by Jesus-followers in the first century CE. As such, it participates as one of the many-faceted expressions of Second Temple Judaism, expressions that consistently wrestled with questions of *how* to be faithful to the God of Israel in the midst of a Gentile-dominated world. The Jesus-followers responsible for and listening to the Gospel of Matthew answered these questions with their fundamental belief that Jesus of Nazareth was God's Christ, whose miraculous birth came as the fulfillment of God's carefully, if surprisingly, orchestrated plan. The surprising rejection, death, and resurrection of Jesus, then, is a continuation of this plan, showing God still acts in ways contrary to expectation.

Belief in Jesus's messianic identity is at the center of Matthew's debates with other Jewish groups, both in the Gospel itself, and in its post–70 CE context. Matthew's Jesus does not disagree with other Jewish schools of thought on foundational elements of Jewish expression such as monotheism, valuing the Torah, and showing faithfulness by loving God and neighbor. Instead, disagreements center on Jesus's identity, and how Jesus's identity shapes his relationship to and interpretation of Scripture. For Matthew's Gospel, Jesus's being God's Christ and Son means that the scriptural story of Israel points to him, just as Matt 1:1–17 demonstrates. So crucial is Jesus's birth that Matt 1:23 gives him the name "Immanuel," or "God with us." For Matthew, Jesus is the hermeneutical key for interpreting all of Scripture, which the Gospel repeatedly emphasizes with fulfillment quotations. From the Gospel's perspective, Jesus has been given "all authority in heaven and earth," and he remains with his disciples through his teaching and through their evangelizing activities to "all the nations"—so much so that the Gospel ends with Jesus's words echoing 1:23: "And remember, I am with you always, to the end of the age" (28:20).

Matthew's focus on Jesus's messiahship is, therefore, the reason for its negative characterization of Jewish religious leaders. Indeed, this claim may reflect continuing conflicts present within Matthew's late first-century context. When reading the Gospel today, we need to be careful to contextualize this story within the debates and varieties of Jewish expressions in the Second Temple period and beyond. Rather than assuming Judaism and Christianity were separate from the start, or worse, that Jesus came to start a new religion, we should reflect on the complicated realities of the ancient Roman world, particularly for Jews who lived as a marginal monotheistic group in the midst of a dominating polytheistic culture. We cannot hope to understand Matthew's story well without keeping this context in mind. If we ignore it, we risk repeating the same mistakes from the past by using the words of a Jewish prophet against his own people. No matter our perspectives on Jesus's identity, we should be able to see the flaws in that.

4

Luke's Story, Part 1

The Gospel as a Message of Inclusion

THE GOSPEL OF LUKE IS the first of two volumes, both traditionally credited to Luke, the physician and traveling companion of
Paul named in Col 4:14. The first volume is similar to Matthew and
Mark, since the author uses at least Mark, and perhaps Matthew
also, as a major source for composition. The Gospel of Luke retells
the story of Jesus's life, the third of the three Synoptic Gospels that
are probably feeling very familiar to you at this point! The second
volume is quite different, however, because it tells the stories of
Jesus's disciples *after* his death and resurrection. The book of
Acts, as it is called, will occupy our attention in the next chapter;
its parallels with the Gospel of Luke show it to be intentionally
connected, but its differences also show how our author, or authorial community, composed when not strictly adhering to source
materials.

This chapter focuses on Luke's Gospel, highlighting its emphasis on including all people, especially the socially marginalized,
in the Kingdom of God. This Gospel includes stories of Jesus
healing or interacting with explicitly outcasted individuals, like
the sinful woman of 7:36–50 and Zacchaeus in 19:1–10; Jesus
does not prohibit his disciples from ministering to Gentiles (9:1–
5; cf. Matt 10:5–6); and more women appear than in any other
Gospel. Luke details not only Mary's perspective on her miraculous pregnancy, for example, but also the reactions of her "relative" (*syngenis*) Elizabeth, the mother of John the Baptist (Luke

An Introduction to the Gospels and Acts. Alicia D. Myers, Oxford University Press. © Oxford University Press 2022. DOI: 10.1093/oso/9780190926809.003.0004

1:24–58). Luke's depiction of Jesus's compassion for marginalized people, combined with the negative characterizations of the rich and powerful, make it a perfect text to combine with a closer look at aspects of identity in the Roman world such as class, gender, ethnicity, and disabilities.[1] Like contemporary Western society, Romans had a hierarchy of these traits that reinforced the status of those in power. Luke's Gospel, however, both uses and subverts this hierarchy in its story of Jesus. While God's Kingdom is still a kingdom in Luke, its subjects are not the rich who have always occupied positions of power, but the outcasts, who accept God's reign while the elite reject it (14:15–24).

CONTEXTUALIZING THE COMPOSITION

The Basics: Authorship, Date, and Location

As mentioned above, Luke, Paul's traveling companion and "beloved physician," is the traditional author of this Gospel and Acts. There is nothing in these writings, however, that mark them as coming from a physician, nor is there an explicit attribution to Luke. Like the other canonical Gospels, this Gospel is anonymous, but I will call it and its author "Luke" for ease of reference. This doesn't mean that our author is completely unidentifiable, though: rhetoric and style show the author to be well educated, at least a God-fearer[2] if not actually Jewish, and a second- or third-generation Christian rather than an eyewitness of Jesus.

Luke writes to someone named "Theophilus," whose identity likewise remains a mystery. Earlier scholars argued that Theophilus could be a stand-in for any believer since the name means "lover of God." While the Gospel and Acts surely had more than one person as an audience, more recent interpreters suggest Theophilus was a wealthy patron who sponsored Luke's project, leading Luke to dedicate both works to him (Luke 1:3; Acts 1:1).[3] Such relationships were common in the Roman world, and authors often honored patrons with dedications. This dedication, therefore, is just one clue that our author is educated, at least through what we would consider secondary levels today. The formal prologue of Luke 1:1–4 reflects rhetorical training, as does the rest of the Gospel, with a wide-ranging vocabulary and awareness of genre expectations for biographical and historiographical narratives.

Luke's education has been used to support the view that he was a Gentile who wrote to other Gentiles. As early as the second century, Papias reflected the tradition that Luke was a native of Antioch (Eusebius, *Eccl. hist.* 3.4). Being from Antioch does not, however, mean that Luke was a Gentile, although it does not preclude it either. Instead, Luke's deep knowledge of the OT as well as his interest in Jewish practices indicates his connection to Jewish thought in his era. His concern for Gentiles also does not require him to be a Gentile, since many Jewish groups looked for Gentile inclusion as a sign of God's Kingdom beginning at least in the writings of Isaiah. Moreover, if we just focus on Gentile inclusion, we miss Luke's consistent interest in the restoration of Israel also present in his writings.[4]

Regardless of Luke's occupation and ethnicity, he was not an eyewitness of Jesus, but received the tradition "handed on to us by those who from the beginning were eyewitnesses and servants of the word" (1:2). Some of these traditions were writings, accounts that "many have undertaken to set down," such as the Gospels of Mark and Matthew. Luke nevertheless emphasizes the trustworthiness of his account, perhaps even indicating its superiority because of his careful investigation and explicit intent to write an "orderly account" (1:1, 3). Although "orderly account" seems ambiguous to us, the Greek word is *diēgēsis*, often translated simply as "narrative." In rhetorical terms, a narrative is a specific genre of writing, one that was expected to be clear, concise, and credible. Luke's use of this technical term, along with the elevated language of his prologue, could imply he sees his version as the best to date.[5]

Luke's use of other sources means this Gospel also postdates the destruction of Jerusalem. Most scholars date the Gospel to the same time as Matthew, somewhere between 80 and 100 CE, and locate it in an urban center outside of Jerusalem; Antioch, Caesarea, Corinth, Ephesus, and Rome have been suggested. The variety of possibilities could be a result of Luke's interest in reaching a wider audience.[6] Incorporating sources from various contexts, Luke crafts a two-volume story that provides an overarching account of God's continuing activity for Israel and all nations. As a result, these volumes depict people from diverse backgrounds, Jewish and Gentile, and from different places throughout the Roman Empire (especially if we include Acts). Luke-Acts, therefore, is not just a biography about Jesus, but a history of how God fulfills promises by bringing salvation to the "end of the earth" (Acts 1:8; cf. Luke 2:31–32). For Luke, salvation comes through the person and work of Jesus, the Christ and Son of God, who demonstrates the ideals of God's Kingdom and trains his disciples to follow in his footsteps once he departs.

Digging Deeper: Intersections of Identity in the Roman World

Hierarchies were ubiquitous in Greco-Roman antiquity. These hierarchies generally reinforced structures of power, reifying current leadership in the name of stability and divine right. The Roman Empire, for example, claimed the emperors were divinely appointed to establish the will of the gods on earth. As divine representatives, and even divine sons, emperors were called the fathers of the country and were to run the empire, just as the male head of the household (paterfamilias) was to run his estate. This system assumes the superiority of the male, manifested best in so-called masculine ways: control, protection, and impenetrability along with the ability to penetrate, or dominate, those lesser than oneself. Those who were biologically male were not necessarily recognized as masculine; thus we should not to assume all male persons were considered superior to all female ones.[7] Only males who had the ability to choose (i.e., free men and patresfamilias) and did choose to live in socially construed masculine ways were superior. Women, children, and slaves were all lesser than the paterfamilias in a household, but hierarchies existed even within lower, feminized roles. Social class distinguished noblewomen from peasants and slaves; sons of nobles were raised to become Roman men who would control their own estates; freeborn and freed persons had patron-client relationships, pledging loyalty to powerful men and women in return for favors and provision; and slaves, too, had hierarchies depending on labor even though they were unable to gain honor for anyone except their masters.

As scholars note, these competitive systems resulted in a very few at the top and the vast majority beneath.[8] Portrayed in Table 4.1, superior and inferior traits were recognized throughout society, and adjusted depending on one's subgroup.[9]

This list does not capture the many middle-range traits or the nuanced combinations of them reflected in people's lives. One could be a free person but a merchant, for example, thus outranking a slave but not a nobleman. Identities are not formed from one trait alone, but through complex intersections of them. Because the construction of identities is complicated and ever-changing, they are better seen as intersections across different spectrums than as a set of strict binaries. At the same time, the extremes demonstrate

Table 4.1

HIERARCHY OF TRAITS IN THE ROMAN EMPIRE

Trait	Superior	Inferior
Citizenship/ethnicity	Roman	Non-Roman
Sex	Male	Female
Gender	Masculine	Feminine
Social class	Free	Slave
Resources	Rich	Poor
Appearance	Symmetrical	Asymmetrical
Physical ability	Able-bodied	Disabled

a preference for those with power to exercise control over themselves and others. For those who were able, conveying control as much as was appropriately possible was the goal.

While some traits were more stable than others (e.g., sex, resources), others changed over a lifetime (e.g., physical ability, appearance), and all were constantly available for external evaluation. Since so much depended on the opinions of others watching lives performed, very few people benefited entirely from these binaries. Emperors, therefore, worked to be masculine, able-bodied, physically beautiful, rich, and so on to evoke the epitome of "being Roman" for the empire. Given this context, we understand better why Julius Caesar regularly wore a laurel wreath to hide his receding hairline; it was part of his masculine performance.[10] The statue of Augustus in Figure 4.1 illustrates these ideals with a militaristic focus: Augustus is dressed as a conqueror, postured in a victorious stance, muscular and symmetrical, and protecting Rome's future as represented by the infant at his feet.[11]

Representations of these traits in material culture such as statues, altars, frescos, and coins show their pervasiveness in the Roman world. These images were effective because they were recognizable and agreed upon. Even non-Romans, who may have defined superior traits differently (e.g., Jews would rank being a Jew better than being a Gentile), nevertheless retained the core system (e.g., being masculine is better than feminine, etc.) and understood Rome's take on them.

Challenging binaries was not only difficult, but also dangerous. It was difficult because while few people benefited from them entirely, most people perceived benefits for themselves in some ways: a man considered himself superior to women and children; a noblewoman benefited from her social status; an educated slave was more valuable than an agricultural laborer; slaves and clients of wealthy patrons received favors from them; free persons were not slaves; and so on (cf. Luke 18:9–14). It was dangerous because the binaries benefited those at the top the most. Aristocratic families retained an overwhelming majority of resources, which

FIGURE 4.1 Augustus of Prima Porta. Statue. Vatican Museums. Public
Domain. Wikimedia Commons.

were funneled to them by slaves, laborers, merchants, and oppressive taxation. Wealthy families offered scraps to retain the loyalty of those dependent upon them, creating numerous patron-client relationships to increase honor and power. Acts of patronage justified aristocratic monopolization of wealth; the rich were educated and, supposedly, knew the best ways to use resources for social betterment. They were portrayed as blessed and divinely chosen to distribute wealth. In reality, these acts perpetuated oppression as aristocratic families worked to secure and grow their wealth at the expense of the poor whom they claimed to protect.[12]

In the Roman world, hierarchies were built on an assumption of scarcity: there is only so much to be had, so I must work for myself and my household to get as much as I can! Every bit I get, the more entrenched I become. "If only I can get a little more," I think. This perspective encourages me to give only to those from whom I expect a return, either materially or socially, and I hoard the rest, fearful of losing the little I have. The Roman Empire benefited from this system that kept people in line, reluctant or unable to challenge it. The emperor was at the top and achieved godlike status as the one who gave food and livelihoods, provided protection, and secured additional resources through conquest for his friends and subjects. In Roman society, economics, culture, and expressions of faith often worked to keep the rich wealthy and the powerful in control. Even though Rome needed those it considered inferior to build and perpetuate itself, it emphasized the superiority of the few at its constructed pinnacle to maintain peace.

The Hospitality of God's Kingdom in Luke (and Acts)

Luke and Acts were written in this larger context, and, accordingly, these writings assume cultural constructions even as it subverts them. As in Mark and Matthew, Luke does not envision an egalitarian utopia; instead, the good news remains the coming of God's Kingdom, which replaces Roman (and all other human) rule in the world. For Luke, God's reign is perfect in part because of its inclusiveness. Unlike Roman patron-client systems that kept the poor cut off from the resources they both produced and needed for survival, Luke's vision of God's Kingdom prioritizes the poor and those otherwise left out of Roman-era constructions of worth, though not as completely as contemporary readers might want.[13] Read as a story from the late first century, however, Luke portrays God's Kingdom as one of divine hospitality. In God's Kingdom everyone relies on God's provision and, therefore, God's evaluation of worth.

Hospitality was highly valued in the Greco-Roman world. It was risky for those who offered it because hospitality (*xenia*) was most often given to strangers (lit. "foreigners," *xenioi*) traveling away from home. This risk also made it valuable because it was very much needed. While inns did exist in larger cities, they were not desirable accommodations and were unavailable in smaller towns. People needed hospitality from others whenever they traveled, especially to places where they had no existing relationships. Hospitality could also initiate powerful and profitable bonds between host and guest. Guests relied on hosts to provide for and protect them. If able, guests would return favors and establish long-term relationships. Both Greco-Roman and Jewish literature have stories of hospitality that highlight the need to welcome travelers, regardless of their identity and especially if they were strangers. Stories describe divine messengers disguising themselves and seeking hospitality from human hosts. If rebuffed, the gods bring judgment; but when welcomed, they bring blessings.[14]

The patriarch Abraham was the model of hospitality in Jewish contexts, including in Luke and Acts. The story begins in Genesis 12, when God calls Abram to leave his homeland for a land God will show him. God also promises Abram that he will become the ancestor of a "great nation" from whom "all other families of the earth shall be blessed" (12:1–3). In Luke and Acts, this promise forms the foundation for Luke's emphasis on inclusion, both for Abraham's overlooked descendants and for the Gentiles (Luke

13:16, 16:19–30, 19:9; Acts 3:25). Abraham's importance in Luke and Acts also reinforces the theme of hospitality, which is related to that of inclusion. God welcomes all into the Kingdom. Abram, likewise, shows hospitality as part of his faithful trust in God's provision.

After obediently leaving his father, Abram lives as a stranger in Canaan, even though God promised to give his descendants that land. When he flees to Egypt during times of famine, Abram relies on the hospitality of the Egyptians to survive (Genesis 13). Abram knows the precariousness of being a stranger in the land.[15] In Gen 18:1–16, the now-named "Abraham" ("father of many") welcomes three strangers at the oak of Mamre "in the heat of the day." He approaches the strangers and offers to feed them without asking their identities. Abraham gives them the best of what he has: cakes, meat, milk, and cheese, and stands under the tree while the men eat, taking on the role of a servant rather than joining the feast (18:5–8). Since Abraham does not know who the men are, he cannot know if they will be able to pay him back or create a profitable relationship. He gives the best anyway; this is ideal hospitality. In the end, Abraham is blessed when the strangers turn out to be divine messengers who bring good news that he and his wife Sarah will have a son (18:9–16). Abraham trusts God as the source of all his goods and believes God will keep the promise of descendants and land. As a stranger in the land himself, Abraham freely gives hospitality because of his trust in God (cf. Genesis 21–22).

In Abraham's story faithfulness and hospitality are interrelated: hospitality reflects the love extended first by God. Humans are called to replicate that love by showing hospitality to one another. In Genesis, Abraham receives God's promise and obeys out of trust, withholding nothing from God or others. Luke picks up these same themes with Jesus's teachings and actions. In three scenes, Jesus teaches at a meal, having enjoyed the hospitality of a host (Luke 7:36, 11:37, 14:1). Noticing the jockeying for power at these meals, Jesus challenges people to welcome everyone, not just those able to return favors (14:15–24). Those welcomed into

God's Kingdom are not the powerful and rich who rely on their wealth and reputations, but the poor and weak who know they need God's care (7:36–50, 12:13–34, 18:9–30). For Luke, this is one reason why it is so hard for the rich and self-righteous to enter God's Kingdom! The poor, sinful, and broken turn to God and receive hospitality because they know they need it, just as Abraham did as a stranger in Canaan. In contrast, the wealthy are invested in a system of hierarchies they trust more than God (16:13), and they are not willing to give up possessions and power without knowing if they will receive a return (18:18–25). As recipients of divine hospitality, however, Jesus teaches his disciples to give freely rather than count superior and inferior traits or look for material rewards (14:25–33; Acts 2:43–47, 4:32–5:11).

LITERARY OVERVIEW

Luke's Gospel relies on Mark, and possibly also Matthew, but it is also its own story. As mentioned above, Luke begins with a formal prologue in 1:1–4.

> Since many have undertaken to set down an orderly account of the events that have been fulfilled among us, just as they were handed on to us by those who from the beginning were eyewitnesses and servants of the word, I too decided, after investigating everything carefully from the very first, to write an orderly account for you, most excellent Theophilus, so that you may know the truth concerning the things about which you have been instructed.

From this prologue, we see Luke's adherence to some literary standards of his day and, therefore, his education. Although the rest of the Gospel does not contain the elevated style of these opening verses, Luke shows his capability here. Moreover, he reveals his intentions and method: he is an investigator and author, not just a cataloger repeating what was already known. The Gospel retells many stories from Mark and Matthew, but it also rearranges them, shortens some, expands others, removes parallels, changes Jesus's speech to be more rhetorically nuanced, and includes otherwise unknown events and perspectives.[16]

The erudition of Luke's prologue also creates his authorial audience, regardless of Theophilus's true identity. This Gospel is written with an educated reader in mind and is meant to reinforce belief rather than evangelize. This final point is probably true of all the NT Gospels, even though they have also been used to evangelize. These writings preserve teachings from and for early believers. This also means Luke, like the other Gospels, is meant to persuade. Unlike Mark and Matthew, however, Luke is explicit about his intentions. He writes so that Theophilus "may know the truth concerning the things about which you have been instructed" (1:4). The "truth" (*asphaleian*) here is not an objective or unattached reporting of events, but an interpretation of "the events that have been fulfilled among us" (1:1). Luke believes Jesus's birth, life, death, resurrection, and ascension to be the fulfillment of God's salvific promises for the people of Israel and the nations of the earth. It is the fulfillment of God's promise made to Abraham so long ago. When Luke tells this story, he seeks to do so in a compelling way.

Luke's story proceeds in the chronological order of Jesus's life while grouping together thematic sayings, just as Mark and Matthew do. Yet Luke also contains a significant amount of additional material fleshing out Jesus's life, including events proceeding his birth, Mary's perspective on her pregnancy, and stories from Jesus's childhood. Luke also shares unique parables, a lengthy travelogue recording Jesus's journey to Jerusalem, more elaborate resurrection stories, and the only explicit account of his ascension in the canonical Gospels. These additions explain Luke's length despite the Gospel's tendency to remove parallels from Mark's account.

The outline below traces Luke's plot and reveals the central place of Jesus's travel to Jerusalem which occupies the bulk of the story:

Beginnings and preparation for ministry (1:1–4:13)
 Prologue (1:1–4)
 Miraculous beginnings (1:5–2:52)
 From John to Jesus (3:1–4:13)

Jesus's ministry in Galilee (4:14–9:50)
 Starting in Nazareth (4:14–30)
 Disciples in training: teachings and healings (4:31–9:6)
 Identifying Jesus (9:7–50)

Turning to Jerusalem: the journey (9:51–19:37)
 Training continues: faithfulness versus hypocrisy
  (9:51–13:9)
 True hospitality: healings and parables (13:10–17:10)
 God exalts the humble (17:11–19:27)

Ministry in Jerusalem (19:28–23:56a)
 Arrival in Jerusalem (19:28–48)
 Teaching in and about the temple (20:1–21:38)
 Jesus's death (22:1–23:56a)
 Jesus's resurrection, teaching, and ascension
  (23:56b–24:53)
  Recognition stories (23:56b–24:43)
  The commission and ascension (24:44–53)

Luke begins his story before Jesus's birth, providing a narrative of John the Baptist's birth (1:5–80) before describing Jesus's early life (2:1–20). In addition to his birth, Luke tells anecdotes of Jesus as a child in the Jerusalem temple (2:21–52), as well as stories of John's ministry, Jesus's baptism, and his testing in the wilderness (3:1–4:13). These beginnings establish the themes that are developed throughout Jesus's ministry, including during the extensive travelogue in 9:51–19:27. Among them is the exaltation of the humble, especially of the poor, alongside the humbling of the proud and wealthy (1:51–55).

Jesus's focus on the marginalized is part of the themes of hospitality and faithfulness described above. Jesus decries hypocrisy in his teaching, while emphasizing faithfulness and obedience. Luke is particularly adamant that faithfulness is shown through giving away earthly possessions and prestige in obedience to God. Questions of wealth and poverty appear regularly in Luke, such as in the adjustment of Matthew's Sermon on the Mount. In Luke, Jesus gives a sermon on the plain, a level place that all people can reach, and he blesses those who are literally poor, hungry, and weeping rather than those who are only so metaphorically (Luke 6:20–26; Matt 5:3–12). These themes also appear in Luke's unique parables, including the Parables of the Good Samaritan in 10:25–37, the Prodigal Son in 15:11–32, and the Rich Man and Lazarus in 16:19–30.[17]

Jesus epitomizes his teachings in his life, especially when he willingly dies as an innocent martyr, the victim of an unjust Roman Empire (23:47–48). Luke's final unique stories are lengthy resurrection scenes, where Jesus explains how his suffering and resurrection fulfills Scripture (24:44–49). For Luke, despite all appearances of power and control that Rome and its allies maintain, God alone orchestrates history. God's control means that disciples should follow God's valuation of worth, rather than the hierarchical systems that disenfranchise the vast majority of people in the Roman world. Jesus's resurrection and ascension in Luke vindicate Jesus, showing his life and interpretation of God's will to be correct. The Gospel ends with Jesus's ascension, but the story continues in the book of Acts, where the disciples seek to live out this new way of life.

KEY PASSAGES AND THEMES

A New Old Story: Pregnant Prophets and Muted Men (Luke 1:5–58)

Luke's Gospel is unique from the very beginning. In addition to the prologue, Luke offers a detailed accounting of two angelic visitations—one to a priest named Zechariah as he served in the Jerusalem temple, and one to an unmarried girl in the small Galilean town of Nazareth, far to the north of Jerusalem and God's holy presence in the temple. In both scenes, the angel Gabriel brings news of upcoming births, and he is met with some incredulity (1:18, 34). These two scenes function as part of Luke's extended comparison between Jesus and John the Baptist. In Greco-Roman rhetoric, comparisons (or *synkrises*) were commonly used to elevate subjects being praised.[18] In this case, Luke compares Jesus to John the Baptist, emphasizing that while John is good and has similar divinely orchestrated origins as Jesus, Jesus is far superior. At the same time, while Jesus's superiority is clear in the narrative, this superiority comes by surprising means.

Right after the prologue, Luke launches into the story of a barren, but righteous, couple named Zechariah and Elizabeth. Those well versed in Scripture should recognize the resonance with the story of Abraham and Sarah and, therefore, anticipate divine intervention leading to a child. Zechariah, we are told, is a priest, and Elizabeth is from the high-priestly line of Aaron (1:5). Both are "righteous before God, living blamelessly according to all the commandments and regulations of the Lord," but they are childless and elderly (1:6). Like Abraham, Zechariah serves God and is rewarded by an angelic messenger who promises a child (1:13–17). Like Sarah, however, he does not believe the news: "How will I know that this is so? For I am an old man and my wife is getting on in years" (1:18; cf. Gen 18:12). Zechariah's request for a sign seems well founded, just as Sarah's incredulity was. Yet, unlike Sarah, Zechariah should have known God has worked miracles like this before; stories of God intervening to cause pregnancies are common in Israel's traditions (Gen 30:22–24; Judg 13:3; 1 Sam 1:3–20). This blameless priest stumbles, and his sign reflects it: he is silenced (Luke 1:19–20). Rebuked, Zechariah shows himself repentant by returning to Elizabeth and going "to his home," a euphemism for having sex with his wife (1:23).[19] God, too, is faithful. Elizabeth conceives and now speaks for herself: "This is what the Lord has done for me when he looked favorably on me and took away the disgrace I have endured among my people" (1:25; cf. Gen 30:22).

Mary's story parallels that of Zechariah and Elizabeth but with some important distinctions. She is far from the temple, in an insignificant town in Galilee; she is a girl, not yet married into the house of David; and we never hear if she lived righteously or blamelessly, like Zechariah and Elizabeth. Instead, Gabriel shows up and tells her she is "favored" by God anyway (Luke 1:28). Like Zechariah, Mary questions Gabriel's news that she will have a son, but her question seems better founded. While God may have remembered barren women and opened wombs in the past, there is no story of a virgin conceiving in Israel's history. Zechariah and Elizabeth both participate in the conception and birth of John, but Joseph is *entirely absent* from Mary and Jesus's story.[20] Mary, thus, is not rebuked for her question, but receives an explanation: "The Holy Spirit will come upon you, and the power of the Most High will overshadow you; therefore the child to be born will be holy; he will be called the Son of God" (1:36). Mary's sign is Elizabeth's pregnancy, but before seeing her relative, Mary consents: "Here I am, the slave of the Lord; let it be with me according to your word" (1:38, my translation).

At this point in the story, it is clear that Jesus is greater than John, in spite of John's miraculous conception and birth. Jesus's conception is the result of direct divine intervention: the Holy Spirit breathes life into Mary's womb just as the Spirit spoke at the moment of creation (Gen 1:1–3).[21] Jesus is not just a prophet; he is God's Son. Jesus's greatness collides with the unusual prophets who proclaim it in the next scene: first, Elizabeth explicitly states that Jesus is greater than the son she carries in 1:41–45; and second, Mary gives a lengthy speech in 1:46–55 that not only confirms Elizabeth's words, but foreshadows the rest of the Gospel. Rather than quoting the OT directly, Mary's words imitate the style of OT prophecies and allude to events from Israel's past, especially the Abrahamic promise. She does not mention Jesus by name, or even her pregnancy, but she proclaims that God's promises are realized after and through these events. These promises are not for a spiritual rescue from sins, but are, instead, God's turning the world upside down by exalting the humble and humbling the exalted (1:51–55). The opening of the Gospel of Luke, therefore, not only tells its readers that God is unsettling the status quo but shows them through those who exemplify this radical shift: an elderly woman and a young girl announce the culmination of God's salvific story with their words, and bring it forth through their bodies (1:57–59, 2:5–7) while their husbands are muted or left out altogether.

Jesus's Mission and Minor Characters in Luke

As in the other Synoptic Gospels, Jesus begins his mission in Luke after being anointed by the Holy Spirit and tested in the wilderness. In each Gospel, Jesus's first actions after these events set the tone for his ministry and interactions with minor characters. In Luke, Jesus travels back to Galilee before preaching and being rejected in his hometown of Nazareth (4:14–30). Luke's Jesus does not preach a series of sayings, as in Matthew, but instead reads from a scroll of Isaiah passed to him during a synagogue service. Jesus stands and reads aloud before offering his interpretation. Although the passage seems to come from just one section of Isaiah, it is actually a combination of two passages (Isa 61:1–2 and 58:6), woven together by Luke as a synopsis of Jesus's mission in this Gospel. Finding his place in the scroll, Jesus reads:

The Spirit of the Lord is upon me, because he has anointed me to bring good news to the poor. He has sent me to proclaim release to the captives, and recovery of sight to the blind, to let the oppressed go free, to proclaim the year of the Lord's favor. (Luke 4:18–19)

Returning to his seat, Jesus begins his interpretation: "Today this scripture has been fulfilled in your hearing" (4:21). While we might be surprised at the boldness of Jesus's claim, those in the synagogue with him rejoice! They had already heard about his deeds from other places in Galilee, and they are excited to receive these powerful promises as well (4:22–23). Jesus, however, has set up a trap for his audience. Jesus repeats the promises they have looked forward to and assures them that God is fulfilling those promises now through him, but the fulfillment is not going to look like what they expected. Just as Jesus's birth stories challenged the status quo, so will the work of Jesus's life.

As Jesus continues interpreting, he connects Isaiah's promises to other events from Israel's past. In what is the first of several comparisons between Jesus's ministry and those of Elijah and Elisha, Jesus describes God's use of these prophets to provide miracles for Gentiles: first, an impoverished widow in Sidon; and, second, a wealthy general from Syria (4:24–27; 1 Kgs 17:1–16; 2 Kgs 5:1–14). In both cases, Jesus emphasizes that God chose to provide food for a widow and heal the leprous Syrian general even though there were many Israelites suffering from these same afflictions at the time. It is at this moment that the crowd in the synagogue turns on Jesus; "filled with rage," they take him to a cliff in order to throw him off (Luke 4:28–29). Jesus, however, easily escapes the crowd, miraculously passing through them to continue on his journey and perform his miraculous deeds elsewhere (4:30–44).

Luke's story demands we consider an important question: why did the crowd react as it did *and* when it did? Common readings often suggest Jewish ethnocentrism is to blame, but this is an unhelpful oversimplification that does not reflect Jesus's repeated healings of Jews in Luke. Instead, it is important to realize what Jesus is saying: not only will miracles go to other people, but even to those who may have wronged you, while you remain in need. As Jesus says, there were lots of widows needing help in Israel, but God did not help them during the famine; and there were many lepers, but God healed an enemy general instead! The reaction of the people of Nazareth is understandable, even if it is extreme: how can God's promises be fulfilled but experienced only by other people? It is not as though the people of Nazareth didn't need help too. Yet this is exactly Jesus's point in Luke: God's Kingdom prioritizes the needs of others over the needs of one's self or one's household. If people were left to choose where God acted, God's reach would be small indeed; God's Kingdom would look a lot like Rome. Just as Elijah and Elisha were pushed to go elsewhere, so too is Jesus; and those who attempt to limit his reach are repeatedly disappointed and condemned (e.g., 4:31–44).

The program of healing and release described in Jesus's reading of Isaiah is a helpful way to view his interactions with minor characters in the remainder of Luke. Being filled with the Holy Spirit (1:35–36, 3:21–22, 4:1, 14–15, 10:21), he preaches to the poor (4:18, 6:20, 7:22, 14:13, 21, 16:20–22, 18:22, 19:8, 21:3), releases people from diseases and demonic possessions (5:11–24, 7:47–49, 13:10–17), and heals the blind (6:39, 7:21–22, 14:13, 21, 18:35–43). When John the Baptist sends disciples to question Jesus about his mission and identity, Jesus responds with a paraphrase of Isaiah again in Luke 7:18–22 and reminds the disciples what they have seen him do. Jesus's actions show who he is.

Shortly following the exchange between Jesus and John's disciples, Jesus demonstrates his mission once again during a meal at Simon the Pharisee's house (7:36–50). This is Jesus's first meal at a religious leader's home, but he has already been questioned about his eating with "tax collectors and sinners" (5:27–38). In 5:29–32, Jesus ate at Levi's home after calling this tax collector to join him as a disciple. In 7:36–50, Jesus welcomes the extreme display of hospitality offered to him by a woman who was a "sinner" (7:39).[22] While tradition often assumes this woman was a prostitute, there is nothing in the story to demand she is guilty of sexual sins. Instead, she is better seen as the second character in a pair in Luke's Gospel, which often sets a man and a woman side-by-side as examples. In this case, she is the female counterpart to Levi, mentioned above, as well as to the paralyzed man brought to Jesus by his friends in 5:17–26.

As in Luke 5:17–26, the Pharisees puzzle over Jesus's claim to be able to forgive sins in 7:46–50. In 5:20–26, Jesus demonstrates his ability to forgive by also curing the paralyzed man, giving life to what would have been understood as his dead legs. Both acts— forgiving sins and giving life—belong to God alone. Jesus's performance of them emphasizes his authority as God's representative agent, God's king, who was anointed by the "Spirit of the Lord" (4:19). Jesus's ministry focuses on the marginalized not because they are inherently more worthy, but because they open themselves up to receive his gifts through vulnerability and humility, two stances that were considered weak in the Roman world. For Luke, participating in God's Kingdom means giving up Roman-era values, regardless of potential social, economic, and even physical costs, because of the gifts one receives in return: forgiveness and eternal life (10:25–42, 18:18–30). God gives better gifts than any human can, even the emperor (11:1–13).

Jesus's Departure: Inaugurating the Kingdom of God

Jesus arrives in Jerusalem in Luke 19:38. After his mock triumph, he begins teaching openly in the temple before being arrested on the night of the Passover meal in 22:47–53. The tension of Jesus's encounters with religious and political leaders throughout the Gospel comes to a head in these final chapters, and, by all outward appearances, the forces allied with Rome seem to win. Jesus is arrested, convicted, and crucified; this would-be insurrectionist is executed. Yet, as in the other Synoptic accounts, Luke also portrays Jesus's death as a moment of victory, where God's providence is shown sovereign. This victory is then reinforced in Jesus's resurrection, his extended teaching scenes, and his ascension in Luke 24. In this final section of the Gospel, Luke lays bare Rome's fear over threats to its rule even as the Gospel also shows Rome's claims of sovereignty to be false. Setting Roman values in contrast to those of God's Kingdom, Luke 19:38–24:53 brings the Gospel's message full circle. Luke emphasizes that while Rome (and those allied with Rome) may think they are in control, their actions come from fear and false understandings of power and worth. Instead, it is God who orchestrates events, even when they are difficult to understand and to face, such as the unjust death of Jesus.

Throughout this section, Luke shows Rome and its allies working to maintain an unjust system that ultimately finds itself aligned with Satanic influence. Indeed, picking up the theme of diabolic interference and temptation from Luke 4:1–13, Judas is persuaded by Satan in 22:3 to play a part with the "chief priests and scribes" hoping to cause Jesus's death. As the story continues, Judas works with these religious leaders to scheme behind the scenes and ultimately arrest Jesus at night, when no crowd could prevent it (22:53). Before Pilate, Jesus is accused of sedition, a charge that explicitly hits on Rome's true fears: loss of tax revenue (23:2–5; cf. 20:22). Even though Pilate, along with Herod (Antipas), knows these charges are false, he renders an unjust verdict (23:14). He releases an actual insurrectionist and murderer in order to appease a crowd by executing an innocent man (23:18–25). Moreover, Rome conscripts another innocent man, Simon of Cyrene, into the act by forcing him to carry Jesus's cross (23:26)! Jesus's innocence is emphasized again as one of the criminals crucified with him defends him (23:39–43), and even the Roman centurion who helped crucify them declares, "Surely this man was innocent" after Jesus's death (23:47). Rome's kingdom is shown to be wholly inept. It worships money, knowingly convicts the innocent, and is powerless to sway the people toward righteousness. It is chaos.

In contrast, Jesus's words and actions demonstrate the right-eousness of God's Kingdom, even in the injustice of his death. Set during Passover, the celebration of Jewish liberation from foreign oppression, Jesus repeatedly acts in accordance to the will of God rather than the will of Rome or its allies. He speaks openly in the temple during the day and offers predictions that are fulfilled both within the story itself and within the lifetime of the first Gospel audiences who experienced Jerusalem's destruction in 70 CE (21:5–38). He shows hospitality when he hosts the Passover meal and predicts restoration for Peter, who he knows will soon betray him (22:14–34; cf. 24:13–35). Jesus foretold his coming rejection, death, and resurrection throughout Luke (9:22, 13:33, 17:25, 18:31, 22:37); in these final chapters, he continues relying on his Father through prayer and obedience (22:39–46, 23:46). Because of his trust in God, Jesus knows that he will suffer and die, but also that he will be raised, a reality Luke hopes to convey to his audience with multiple resurrection accounts in Luke 24. God's control, therefore, is made plain by means of Roman pretensions. Although Rome believes itself to reign, its machinations are shown only to fulfill what was already proclaimed in Scripture, by Jesus during his lifetime, and to his disciples after his resurrection.

Overall, then, Luke seeks to encourage its audiences to con-tinue trusting in and living out the ethics of God's upside-down Kingdom. This, we recall, was the intent made clear in Luke's pro-logue, where Theophilus is told the Gospel was written "so that you might know the truth of the things about which you have been taught" (1:4). These "things" are the "events that have been fulfilled among us": namely, Jesus's life, death, and resurrection (1:1). It is not surprising, then, that Luke's Jesus ties his rejection, death, and resurrection to scriptural fulfillment throughout his life and then reveals it in more detail to his disciples after his resur-rection (24:27, 32, 44–49). Luke, like the other canonical Gospels, continues the teaching that the OT can only be rightly under-stood from a post-Easter perspective. Yet Luke, more so than the other Gospels, underscores how God's Kingdom flips the priorities of Roman rule. Jesus's death, the most humiliating and weakest way to die in the Roman world, is presented as heroic and victorious, even "righteous" (23:47).[23] And just as Jesus focused on the marginalized during his life, news of his resurrection does the same: the women are first to hear (24:1–12), followed by two otherwise unknown disciples (24:13–33), and the yet-to-be-restored Peter (24: 34–35), before the rest of the apostles see Jesus (24:36–49). The evaluations of worth in God's Kingdom, therefore, continue to challenge Roman-era values, even among the disciples who don't believe the women who rightly testify to them (24:11, 22)! As the story continues in Acts, the disciples will be "clothed with power," but they will continue to need guidance to let go of Rome's view of the world in order to share the good news of God's victorious inversion of it.

CONCLUSIONS

Finishing our time with Luke means we've come to the end of the Synoptic Gospels. Luke's version aims to be the most comprehensive and most credible of the three, with the formal prologue that guides the rest of the work. We focused on the ways Luke's version expands Jesus's ministerial work for those on the margins, turning upside down the Roman evaluations of worth even while maintaining a hierarchy in God's Kingdom. Luke's presentation of the good news is the coming of God's Kingdom through Jesus, which fulfills promises reaching back to Abraham. This kingdom subverts parts of the Roman world, but it does not create an egalitarian one. Instead, the ranking of traits changes: God is supreme, and Jesus is God's reigning king rather than the Roman emperor; it is better to be a child or slave in God's household than to run your own and acquire wealth; women are truthful proclaimers of God's will as much as men are; and it is easier for the poor and broken to rely on God's deliverance than for the rich and (seemingly) self-sufficient. The goal of the Gospel is to convince the audience to believe in and live out this ethic, regardless of their own life circumstances. Indeed, if Theophilus is a real person wealthy enough to support Luke's project, he (and others like him) can be encouraged that they have reoriented their lives to fit God's Kingdom, like Peter in 18:28–30. They have sacrificed, and Luke's Jesus strengthens them to continue doing so.

When the story resumes in the book of Acts, these themes continue, though with notable tweaks: meals and hospitality, travelogues, and the importance of spreading the good news remain the same. Rather than focusing on Jesus, however, the Spirit becomes the main agent through whom God's will is delivered and enacted. The Gospel of Luke has prepared the disciples and given them the model of Jesus's life; in the book of Acts, the disciples are empowered with God's Spirit to follow through in their own lives. The disciples, though, continue to need challenging, learning repeatedly that God works and speaks through anyone, not just those they deem worthy. The applications of this message in our current world are clear: Luke and Acts emphasize that all humans are valuable simply because they exist. People need to recognize that value when they encounter others, especially those who are usually overlooked and oppressed, as well as when they look at themselves. Picking up with Acts, we will see how God's Spirit keeps pushing the boundaries of God's Kingdom outward, teaching the disciples in the past and acting as a teacher for us now, too, not to discount and dehumanize others regardless of our own faith perspectives.

Luke's Story, Part 2

God's Spirit-Driven Mission in the Book of Acts

THE BOOK OF ACTS IS the second volume of Luke's two-part story. Acts picks up where the Gospel of Luke stops, but with some differences. Luke 24 ties up loose ends with Jesus's ascension and the disciples joyfully returning to Jerusalem to wait to be "clothed with power from on high" (24:49–53). Acts, though, starts by retelling Jesus's time with the disciples before his ascension, making special mention of his remaining with them for forty days to teach them about the kingdom of God (Acts 1:3). Part of this teaching is a clarification of why the disciples are waiting in Jerusalem: they will be baptized with the Holy Spirit "not many days from now" (1:5). Enabled by this Spirit, the disciples are promised they will be Jesus's "witnesses in Jerusalem, in all Judea and Samaria, and to the ends of the earth" (1:8).[1] The disciples then watch Jesus ascend, but do not return to Jerusalem joyfully; they wait with necks arched upward for Jesus to come back. They must be prodded by "two men in white robes" to return and begin preparing for the coming of the Holy Spirit (1:9–11; cf. Luke 24:4). Luke's tidy conclusion to his Gospel is reshaped to become the starting point for Acts.

Most scholars suggest Acts 1:8 lays out the program for this book, tracking the spread of the disciples' witnessing activities geographically: first in Jerusalem (Acts 1–7), then in Judea and Samaria (8–12), continuing to the "end" (*eschatos*) of the earth that

An Introduction to the Gospels and Acts. Alicia D. Myers, Oxford University Press. © Oxford University Press 2022. DOI: 10.1093/oso/9780190926809.003.0005

is Rome (13–28).[2] Yet there is more to this opening scene than just a map for what follows. Jesus promises his disciples baptism with the Holy Spirit and their being his witnesses throughout the earth, but 1:6–11 also indicates they will face obstacles. These obstacles include the disciples themselves, as well as the human expectations of kingdoms that they, and others, assume. According to Acts, the disciples and those to whom they witness need divine intervention in order to reshape and redirect their lives to fulfill God's plan of salvation, especially as communicated in the Abrahamic promise (Gen 12:1–3; Luke 1:55, 73; Acts 3:25). After Jesus's ascension, the Holy Spirit is God's primary agent of intervention, inspiring not only the disciples within the story of Acts, but also connecting centuries of believers listening to Luke's narrative.

CONTEXTUALIZING THE COMPOSITION

The Basics: Authorship, Date, and Location

The questions of context from the previous chapter on the Gospel of Luke remain relevant for Acts. Acts is also traditionally ascribed to Luke, dated anywhere between 80 and 125 CE, and thought to be composed in an urban center such as Antioch of Syria.[3] As before, I will continue to call the author "Luke" for ease of reference; just like Third Gospel, however, Acts too is anonymous. Acts differs from the Gospel by incorporating "we" passages that seem to imply the author's traveling with Paul and his entourage at various points (16:1–17, 20:5–16, 21:1–17, 27:1–28:16). Yet the sporadic nature of these passages and their inconsistency with the Pauline letters lead many to believe they are a narrative device rather than an indication of eyewitness testimony.[4]

Our conclusions about Acts are both clarified and complicated by its connection to the Gospel of Luke: judgments made about the Gospel necessarily impact how we read Acts. Rather than starting with the speculation, let's begin by diving into Acts itself, seeing how 1:1–5 explicitly connects this book back to the Gospel of Luke. Acts begins:

> In the first book, Theophilus, I wrote about all that Jesus did and taught from the beginning until the day when he was taken up to heaven, after giving instructions through the Holy Spirit to the apostles whom he had chosen. After his suffering he presented himself alive to them by many convincing proofs, appearing to them during forty days and speaking about the kingdom of God. While staying with them, he ordered them not to leave Jerusalem, but to wait there for the promise of the Father. "This," he said, "is what you have heard from me; for John baptized with water, but you will be baptized with the Holy Spirit not many days from now."

Several parts of this introduction point us back to the Gospel. First, we learn that Acts is the second of two books. That the "first book" is Luke is indicated by the reintroduction of Theophilus. Theophilus's presence also means we have the same audience (whether constructed or real): Acts is again written to, and its composition possibly also funded by, a wealthy patron named Theophilus, a second- or third-generation believer whom Luke seeks to encourage (Luke 1:4). Theophilus's access to funds again indicates access to education, which is also reflected in Acts' rhetorical shaping and reflection of genre expectations.

Second, Acts opens with a short summary of the Gospel, which focused on "all that Jesus did and taught from the beginning" until his ascension. The Gospel is a biography. Acts changes focus from Jesus to the apostles, whom Jesus promises "will be baptized with the Holy Spirit." The apostles, however, are not the main characters in Acts. Instead, God is the key actor, this time mediating the divine will by the Holy Spirit rather than Jesus.[5] Apostles and disciples participate in God's mission, but not because they are the center of attention; rather, they participate because God "pours out" the Spirit on them (2:17).[6] For this reason, most scholars think Acts is a historiography rather than a biography. To be sure, ancient historiographies are similar to biographies, but the overall emphasis is different. A historiography tracks an event or movement, while a biography conveys the essence of its subject by telling a life story.

Calling Acts a historiography does not mean it is "historically accurate" in the same way we expect modern history textbooks to be. The second-century rhetorician Lucian of Samosata (ca. 120–180 CE) provides instructions for writing historiographies in his *How to Write History*. He argues historiographers should tell the whole story, as best they can, and use impartial and omniscient third-person narrators.[7] Historians also incorporated speeches and dialogues, but these were not verbatim repetitions; instead, as the famous historian Thucydides explains in his *History of the Peloponnesian War*:

> The speeches are given in the language in which, as it seemed to me, the several speakers would express, on the subjects under consideration, the sentiments most befitting the occasion, though at the same time I have adhered as closely as possible to the general sense of what was actually said.[8]

Without recording equipment, this was the best a historian could do. Speeches were credible so long as they were appropriate to the person and the occasion, but they were not expected to be exact. The same rules apply to the description of events; the goal is overall credibility and truthfulness, rather than precise accuracy in contemporary terms.

While surprising to us, ancient historiographies also regularly mention divine intervention such as omens, prophecies, miraculous healings, or deliverance from disasters, alongside more commonplace themes of travel and conflict. We need to remember that most people in the first century (as for many centuries before and after) not only believed in miracles but expected them because they assumed supernatural involvement in everyday life. These supernatural elements include God or gods, but also intermediary angels or *daimonia* (demons), which could be positive, negative, or neutral influences in daily life. As noted in the chapter on Mark's Gospel, ancient people viewed the world as full of spirits, which could possess people for good and for ill. Acts depicts a similar perspective, which reflects its historical context regardless of our own beliefs about supernatural beings. Indeed, if Acts had been devoid of divine interactions, ancient audiences would have found it an impossible tale as well as an odd sequel to the Gospel.

The third way Acts 1 connects back to the Gospel of Luke is Jesus's comment to the disciples. Jesus's promise of the Holy Spirit explicitly references John's baptizing activity from Luke 3. In Luke 3, John's baptism is called "a baptism of repentance for the forgiveness of sins" and tied to a lengthy quotation of Isa 40:3–5. After describing what the "fruits of repentance" should look like in Luke 3:10–14, John foretells a later baptism given by the one coming after him: "He will baptize you with the Holy Spirit and fire" (3:16). *This* is the baptism Jesus promises in Acts 1 and which is fulfilled with the Spirit's coming with "tongues of fire" in Acts 2. John's "baptism of repentance" also resonates with Jesus's resurrection promise to the disciples in Luke 24:47 that they will be witnesses by proclaiming "repentance and forgiveness of sins . . . beginning in Jerusalem." Jesus repeats the promise of being witnesses in Acts 1:8, signaling that we should keep looking for repentance in what follows (more on that below). For all these reasons and more, most scholars argue that Luke-Acts should be read as a single, two-volume work even though it comprises distinctive genres, focuses, and even theological emphases.[9]

Regardless of the details behind Acts' composition, therefore, we can affirm a few things with confidence. Acts is the second volume of Luke's larger project narrating Jesus's life (Gospel) and the life of the movement inspired by him (Acts). Although written later, Acts has the same author and audiences as the Gospel of Luke. Like the Gospel, Acts was written after the destruction of the Jerusalem temple and the traditional dates for the deaths of many first apostles, including Peter and Paul.[10] Acts addresses the question of what Christians should do while they wait for Jesus to come back as promised. The opening scene of Acts pushes believers to trust in and obey Jesus's words rather than stand around with crooked necks waiting for him to descend. Jesus's final words to his apostles are also for Acts' audiences: baptized with the Holy Spirit, they will be witnesses, not only to the geographical limits of the earth, but to its temporal "end" as well.

Digging Deeper: Conversion and Repentance in the Greco-Roman World

In the previous chapter, I discussed how identities were formed and evaluated in the Roman world. In this chapter, I will focus on conversion, or repentance, in the same era. In Acts, repentance plays a key role in the plot. Indeed, one question pervading the book is if people will believe the revelations given through miraculous deeds and speeches from the Spirit-filled disciples. As Luke's story moves from a biography to a historiography, he shifts his focus from one person to the group that person has left behind. Inspired by the Holy Spirit, these disciples begin establishing God's Kingdom on earth, changing their own lives and challenging others to change alongside them. They call people to redirect their lives and participate in a new way of calculating traits through repentance. Rather than conforming to Rome's vision, the disciples call others to follow what Luke calls "the Way" (Acts 9:2).

As we saw in the previous chapter, a person's identity was not associated with only one trait in the Roman world. Instead, an intersection of traits was constantly evaluated by oneself and others, could change over a lifetime, and varied depending on one's contexts. For example, a Roman noblewoman would be identified by her social status of having resources, but also by her gender as a woman, her physical appearance, citizenship, marital status, as well as whether she birthed living children. The complex intersections of traits, as well as the various ways they were evaluated, means pinpointing identity in the first century is a challenging thing to do (just as it is now!).

Even though traits could change over a person's lifetime, most ancient people did not think an individual's fundamental personality, or character (*ēthos*), changed. Rather, they believed one's character was revealed through the topoi introduced at the outset of this book: "origin, nature, training, disposition, age, fortune, morality, action, speech, manner of death, and what followed death."[11] A person's age changes, but ancient Romans did not think a person's *character* did. An elderly man, for example, would not be as physically capable as when he was younger, but if he were a *good* man, he would recognize his diminishing ability and not linger in public life.[12] His age changes, but his goodness remains constant. Likewise, authors often include childhood anecdotes in biographies because a person's character was seen even at a young age. Thus, when Jesus teaches the teachers in the Jerusalem temple at age twelve, we expect he will continue outwitting them as an adult (Luke 2:46–47). He does not disappoint!

When constructing characters, ancient authors include information on topoi to convey the morality of a person's choices, evaluating them as good, bad, or ambiguous. While the Gospel of Luke reveals Jesus's character to inspire the audience to imitate him, Acts is different. As a historiography, it offers short snapshots of people, with topoi still included about each of them, but never as fully as for Jesus in the Gospel. Instead, Acts is more interested in how a cast of characters will respond to God's actions: will they believe and imitate Jesus, or will they remain unrepentant? But written in a context that did not think people *changed*, how could Acts expect any sort of "conversion" in its characters—let alone be able to convince its audiences that change was possible? That's what we'll look at next.

Repentance as Redirection:
Roman-Era Understandings

Although Roman-era authors rarely describe people changing, there are conversion stories in ancient literature. Some conversion stories are easily recognizable to us: a person leaves an old life behind to follow God or gods or a new religious practice. In other stories, students leave old ways and come to a philosopher to learn. In yet others, people recommit to ancestral religious practices. We might identify repentance most easily in the last group of stories, but repentance is involved in all of them when characters *change their minds*; this is what the Greek for "repentance" (*metanoeō*) really means. While people could embark on a totally new faith or practice, repentance/conversion can also be a return to the good. In fact, since ancient people understood the Good to be constant, any conversion to follow the Good is a type of repentance: a return to the right way of thinking and living. Thus, philosophers encouraged young men to repent of mistakes so their souls would be trained to choose the better, OT prophets and NT authors call on the people to repent and turn back to God, and other Jewish stories tell of famous figures repenting, such as Enoch and Manasseh. In all these works, conversion and repentance overlap as a divinely inspired choice made at a crucial moment in life.[13]

The divine inspiration of these profound choices explains the paradox noted above: ancient Jews and Romans believed people could repent or convert when a charismatic individual, God, or a god intervened.[14] A person or group is jarred into self-reflection, or overcome by attraction, to follow a new or renewed way of life. Yet, while changes do take place, there is rarely a fundamental shift in a character's personality after repentance. Instead, this personality is redirected toward a different, better or right, goal. In the Jewish novel *Joseph and Aseneth*, for example, Aseneth's character is not altered, it is redirected. The daughter of an Egyptian priest, Aseneth devotes herself to the Egyptian deities. Extremely chaste and virtuous, she lives at the very top of a high tower adjoining her father's house, surrounded by her idols. She has never spoken to any male, not even a child, before she meets Joseph and is overcome by his handsomeness. Aseneth is an ideal Egyptian girl: chaste and devoted to her gods. When she repents after being visited by the angelic personification of "Repentance" (Metanoia), her devotion does not disappear, but shifts to the God of Israel. Moreover, she famously rejects all other men and remains chaste in her marriage to Joseph.[15] Repentance, therefore, does not change one's personality; it redirects already-established traits in what the story portrays as the *right* direction.

This knowledge matters when we read Acts, which is full of conversion or repentance tales. The entire book focuses on spreading a message to gain adherents. Throughout Christian history, different groups have used Acts to discern a program for evangelistic missions. In fact, for many American Protestants at the beginning of the twentieth century, Acts was a "missions textbook."[16] When we read Acts in light of ancient expectations, however, we see that Luke portrays repentance as a divinely initiated redirection of a person's traits. Moreover, in Acts, imitating Jesus does not automatically require a complete change in one's lifestyle, even when wealthy Gentiles join the movement (Acts 10–28). Instead, the emphasis is on the sheer variety of people called into the movement, regardless of ethnicity, gender, wealth, or occupation.

Repentance and the Way in Acts

Acts repeatedly uses the words "repentance" (*metanoia, metanoeō*) and "turn from" (*epistrephō*) in its conversion tales.[17] In Acts, God breaks into people's lives to call them to a new, or renewed, way of living. The most obvious example is the story of Paul, whose visionary encounter with Jesus is narrated three times in Acts but never with any of the words for repentance (9:1–31, 22:1–21, 26:9–18). Nevertheless, in this story, we find the classic elements of a repentance story: a character is confronted by God and is redirected to follow God's will. Paul is Jewish ethnically as well as in his religious practice (see Chapter 3 for a review of Judaism/s in the first century). When confronted by Jesus, Paul redirects his zealous fervor from persecuting Jesus's disciples, whom he had seen as a threat, to joining them as a witness of Jesus's identity. After his vision, Paul understands Jesus as the fulfillment of God's promises to Israel, rather than a break from them (13:16–52). Paul does not stop being Jewish in order to become a Christian. Rather, he redirects his practices in a way that he believes coheres better with his Jewish identity (22:1–21). Paul repents and joins God's plan as understood in Acts.

In Acts, as in the literary examples above, divine intervention is needed to inspire this redirection of character. God motivates repentance and provides commissions; it is neither self-derived nor private. Paul is engulfed by an overpowering light, but the major divine intervention in Acts occurs earlier, when the Holy Spirit "fills" all the believers gathered in Jerusalem on Pentecost (2:1–4). This "filling" not only fulfills Jesus's promise from Luke 24 and Acts 1, but also indicates a change in time. When Peter explains the Spirit's arrival, he quotes Joel 2:28–32, saying, "In the *last days* it will be, God declares, that I will pour out my Spirit upon all flesh" (Acts 2:17). Recall the discussion of apocalyptic thought from the chapter on Mark's Gospel: here we find this theme again, along with spirit possession (Mark 1:9–11). According to Acts, the arrival of God's Spirit, and its dramatic possession "upon all flesh," is a sign that they are "in the last days." Seeing this moment, the crowd is brought to a crossroads: will they "repent and be baptized" as Spirit-filled Peter commands, or will they remain on their current path (2:38–42)?

Those who do repent are made part of the community of believers, joining the movement Luke refers to as "the Way" (9:2, 18:25–26, 19:9, 23, 22:4, 24:14, 22). The growing diversity of this fellowship will become a major sticking point for believers as Gentiles are incorporated alongside ethnic Jews. As in the Gospel, the Abrahamic promise surfaces as an explanation (Acts 3:25, 13:26), and the Holy Spirit's arrival is confirmation in 10:44–48, with a second outpouring on Cornelius's household. In Acts 10, Peter learns his prophetic words from 2:17 stretch even farther than he thought: all flesh means all flesh (10:34).

Coming along the Way at one moment, however, does not mean believers cannot turn back. Since character traits do not fundamentally change with repentance, but are redirected, they continue to bubble up in the story. Paul remains zealous after he repents, but his stubbornness is in Jesus's service; Peter remains the apostolic spokesperson, but also continues to show fear and runs away in Acts 12 (cf. Luke 22:54–62); and Simon Magus never gets over his desire for fame and fortune (Acts 8:9–24). In Luke's writings, we see which spirit "fills" or possesses characters by following their actions. Those possessed by the Holy Spirit continue as Jesus's witnesses, perform wondrous deeds, and participate in the community. Those who are filled with other spirits, especially diabolical ones, re-enact Judas's betrayal from the Gospel (Luke 22:3, "then Satan entered into Judas"): they turn against other believers, steal resources, or seek power that belongs to God alone (Acts 5:3, 8:20–23). For Luke, repentance and forgiveness are not one-time events, but the result of a continual disposition that leaves believers open to possession by God's Spirit rather than one of the many malevolent ones also present in the world (cf. 19:11–17).

LITERARY OVERVIEW

We previously explored the genre of Acts, as well as its relationship to the Gospel of Luke. In this short literary overview, I will focus on the narrative flow of Acts. As with the previous books we discussed, there are multiple ways to outline Acts. By far the most popular is using Acts 1:8 as a geographical program for the book from Jerusalem (1–7), to Judea and Samaria (8–12), and the end of the earth (13–28). Another popular option is to focus on the main apostolic characters who appear in the story: Acts 1–12 centering on Peter and 13–28 on Paul. Yet another method is to note moments in Acts where the narrative slows down, developing certain characters and conflicts. Acts 1–9 builds to a climactic moment about Gentile inclusion and its implications in Acts 10:1–15:35, while the later portion of the book follows Paul's missionary travels (15:36–25:27), climaxing with his lengthy speech to Herod Agrippa before he finishes his journey to Rome (26–28).[18]

The outline below combines elements of all these approaches while seeking to highlight major points of transition in the narrative. Acts regularly creates what ancient authors called "chain-link" structures, which summarize major points and foreshadow upcoming characters or themes.[19]

Believers in Jerusalem (1:1–8:3)
    Beginnings: promise, preparation, and Pentecost
        (1:1–2:47)
    The Jesus community (3:1–6:7)
    Transition: Stephen and Saul (6:8–8:3)

God continues including others (8:4–12:25)
    Samaritans and an Ethiopian official (8:4–40)
    Saul the persecutor (9:1–35)
    Gentiles and the church in Antioch (9:36–11:30)
    Transition: Peter flees; Barnabas and Saul travel (12:1–25)

Good news to Gentiles outside of Palestine (13:1–21:16)
    It's official: decisions to include Gentiles (13:1–15:41)
    Journeys continue: Paul's new entourage (16:1–20:12)
    Transition: Paul's farewell and foreshadowings of trouble
        (20:13–21:16)

The good news in Rome (21:17–28:31)
    Paul's arrest and testimony in Jerusalem (21:17–23:11)
    Paul in Caesarea: governors, kings, and appealing to the
        emperor (23:12–26:32)
    Transition/conclusion: journey and witnessing in Rome
        (27:1–28:31)

Overall, Acts narrates a geographical movement of the disciples' witnessing activity from Jerusalem to Rome. These disciples are empowered by the Holy Spirit and face various conflicts from within the movement as well as from external Jewish and Gentile groups. Acts has been accused of being anti-Jewish, with some good reason. In their speeches, the disciples blame their Jewish audiences in Jerusalem for Jesus's death (2:22–23, 3:14–15, 7:52–53) and Paul often leaves synagogues (13:44–45, 18:6) and even faces some violent Jewish opposition to his preaching (14:5, 17:5, 11–13). At the same time, however, the disciples who speak in Acts are all ethnically Jewish themselves; they are criticizing fellow Jews in the presence of other Jews, rather than as outsiders. As noted in the chapter on Matthew, social identity theory highlights how people are often harder on those they are close to than they are on outsiders. The picture in Acts is more complicated than the straightforward anti-Judaism that we will see in the Christian Apocrypha. Not all Jews are negative characters in Acts, and they do not always reject Christians, even Paul. Paul collects disciples from synagogues and meets up with Jewish believers in Corinth (18:1–4). At the same time, Gentiles and Roman officials are not singularly positive in Acts. Instead, they regularly oppose disciples, especially Paul (16:16–40, 17:1–8, 19:21–41), and it is the injustice of the Roman system that leads to his arrest. Rather than painting entirely positive or negative portraits of characters, Luke emphasizes it is God who is ultimately orchestrating all events. The disciples' obstacles, whether from Jewish or Gentile sources, mirror Jesus's own, thus showing the disciples to be inspired by the same Holy Spirit as fellow participants in God's plan. In this way, Acts encourages audiences to imitate the disciples' imitations of Jesus by showing them they can face opposition, as well as acceptance, anywhere; it is God who is bringing this plan to completion.

Imitating Jesus's ministry is an important way Acts shows disciples to be authentic and inspired by the Holy Spirit. Throughout Acts, various disciples re-enact healings, fulfill Jesus's words, offer similar teachings, and suffer parallel trials. Perhaps the most apparent of these scenes is Stephen's martyrdom in Acts 7–8. When he dies, Stephen asks Jesus to "receive" his spirit, just as Jesus commends his to the Father in Luke 23:46 (Acts 7:59; cf. Ps 31:6). Like Jesus, Stephen dies an innocent martyr, and his death is a witness to God's plan. This death initiates the movement of Jesus's witnesses outside of Jerusalem in accordance with the promise from 1:8. As Acts continues, more disciples repeat scenes from the Gospel. In Acts 9:36–43, Peter travels to Joppa to heal a disciple named Tabitha. When he arrives, she is already dead, but Peter nonetheless goes to the upper room where her body was laid. He tells all the others to leave, and then raises Tabitha after praying and saying, "Tabitha, get up" (9:40). This story emulates Jesus's raising of Jairus's daughter in Luke 8:40–56. In Acts 20–28, Jesus's long journey to Jerusalem from Luke 9–19 is reimagined in Paul's journey to Jerusalem and then to Rome. Like Jesus, Paul knows his fate but obediently follows the Lord's will even though he has opportunities to escape it. Arrested, Paul fulfills Jesus's words from Luke 21:12–15 when he testifies before "kings and governors" in Acts 22–26.

When Acts ends, it leaves Paul in Rome without the tidiness of Luke 24. According to the *Acts of Paul*, Paul was martyred under Nero around 64 CE. Acts, however, not only ends before Paul's death, but also before he has a chance to speak to the emperor, as he asked to do in 25:11–12. For Acts, the whole reason Paul is in Rome is because he "appealed to Caesar [the emperor]" (25:21, 26:32, 27:24, 28:19)! The absence of this information has led some to suggest a longer ending of Acts has been lost, but it seems better to accept the current ending as it is, not least because we have no manuscript evidence to suggest otherwise.[20] Acts is not a biography of Paul, but a historiography describing how God's message spreads through Spirit-empowered disciples, regardless of human opposition. Paul is an important witness, but he is not the only witness, nor is he the only one to make it to Rome. Instead, all the way back in Acts 2 Jewish travelers from Rome heard Peter's inaugural sermon and witnessed the arrival of the Holy Spirit. Any new believers from this group would have taken the message back when they returned to Rome. Thus, when Paul meets other Jesus-followers from Rome in 18:1–2 and is ministered to by disciples in Rome when he arrives (28:15), it should not be a surprise. When Acts ends with Paul still preaching "without hindrance" in Rome (28:31), it encourages Theophilus and other Christians in the audience to remember their duty to be Jesus's witnesses as well. Jesus has not returned yet; all disciples have a job to do (1:8–11).

KEY PASSAGES AND THEMES

God's Gift: The Spirit and Pentecost

Acts 2 plays a crucial role in the plot of Acts, as well as in the two-volume work of Luke-Acts as a whole. While gathered in prayer in Jerusalem, the believers are filled with the Holy Spirit as a "violent wind" rushes into the room: "divided tongues . . . as of fire rested on each of them" (2:2–3). From this moment onward, the disciples begin their work as Jesus's witnesses in Acts. This scene fulfills Jesus's promises to the disciples in Acts 1, with its links back to Luke 3 and 24 (cf. Luke 11:13). Astute readers will also remember the Holy Spirit's prominent role in Jesus's conception and ministry in the Gospel (1:35, 3:22, 4:1–2, 10:21). Luke makes special mention of the Holy Spirit, including in Jesus's inaugural teaching in Luke 4: "The Spirit of the Lord is upon me, because he has anointed me to bring good news to the poor" (v. 18). As we saw in the previous chapter, Jesus's ministry fulfills this prophetic combination of passages from Isaiah. Jesus, conceived by the Holy Spirit, lives as one animated by this Spirit. Now that his disciples have been similarly anointed in Acts, they too should live in the same way, inspired to act and speak by this same Spirit.

The way the Spirit arrives in Acts is very different from in Luke. In Luke, the Spirit's first actions are in the miraculous pregnancies of Elizabeth and Mary. In Acts, however, the Spirit comes with frightening and befuddling power upon an entire group of praying believers. As scholars note, the picture of a rushing wind and fire is similar to theophanies (God-appearances) in the OT, such as in Exodus when God guides the Israelites with a pillar of fire, or God's presence being signaled by fire and "thunders and lightnings" at Sinai and a cloud with fire in the Tabernacle (Exod 19:16–18, 40:38).[21] The image of "tongues of fire" also appears in the *Aeneid* over Aeneas's son Iulus as a sign of divine election for the future of Rome.[22] Similarly, in Acts, the tongues of fire demonstrate the believers' connection to God as recipients of the Holy Spirit, as well as their special commission as witnesses.

Yet while the image of Acts 2:1–4 sets these believers apart as the first recipients of God's Spirit, Peter's speech informs the confused crowd that they are not the only ones who will receive this gift. In 2:14–40, Peter speaks to the crowd in Jerusalem who had gathered to celebrate Pentecost, a festival that marked fifty days after Passover. Although a festival associated with the wheat harvest in Exodus and Deuteronomy, it also recalled the giving of the Torah at Sinai. Having survived Passover and left Egypt, the Israelites came to Sinai to receive God's instructions for how to live as God's people. At Pentecost, the Jews remembered this event and how it established Israel as God's covenant people. When Peter and the other believers are filled with God's Spirit in Acts 2, they too communicate God's message to the gathered Israelites. Importantly, Peter quotes and interprets Scripture to these Israelites, showing evidence of Jesus's teaching him how his death and resurrection fulfilled Scripture (Luke 24:44–48). In Luke's telling, this moment is as crucial to God's relationship with Israel as Sinai was.

In Acts 2:17–21, Peter quotes from Joel 2:28–32. As mentioned above, this quotation begins, "In the last days it will be, God declares, I will pour out my Spirit upon all flesh." The coming of the Spirit upon all those gathered in prayer, both men and women, fulfills this Scripture and, therefore, prompts a turning of the ages: Acts is situated "in the last days." Peter continues, "Your sons and your daughters will prophesy, and your young ones will see visions and your old ones shall dream dreams. Even upon my slaves, both men and women, in those days I will pour out my Spirit, and they shall prophesy." My translation is a bit different because it highlights the inclusive nature of the quotation. Joel's prophecy is emphatic that *all flesh* really means *all flesh*. Thus, while Peter and the other 120 who were initially filled with the Spirit at Pentecost are the first, they are far from the only ones who receive this anointing. In Acts, we are repeatedly told of characters being "filled" with the Holy Spirit, which indicates their participation in these last days and in God's overarching plan (2:4, 4:8, 31, 6:3, 5, 8, 7:55, 9:17, 11:24, 13:9).

The inclusivity of this prophecy should not be overlooked, but neither should the fact that Acts does not always live up to its own standards of inclusion. We hear no actual prophecy from women believers in Acts despite their noted presence in communities (e.g., Tabitha, Lydia, and Priscilla). And, as in other Roman literature, slave girls are expendable (16:16–18) or the butt of a joke (12:12–17). Indeed, Peter may interpret Joel 2, but he does not understand the implications right away. He must learn that *all flesh* also includes Gentiles, women, young girls, other men and boys, slaves, a persecutor turned colleague, Samaritans, and a eunuch from Ethiopia. While reading Acts, pay attention to how the disciples are continually reminded that God's plan of salvation is always bigger than they imagine.[23] Even Acts itself cannot contain the whole story.

A Message to All People: Fulfilling Abraham's Promise

There are several significant passages in Acts where the disciples learn, sometimes willingly and sometimes with great reservation, that God is indeed including all people in the message and plan of salvation. When we start Acts, the early believers seem quite content to remain in Jerusalem. In spite of the way Acts 1:8 is read as a blueprint for the book, the earliest disciples did not feel any sort of urge pushing them outside Jerusalem. Rather, they witnessed in Jerusalem, and God's message spreads as Pentecost pilgrims head home in Acts 2. Often overlooked by more contemporary readers of Acts, this is the initial spread of the Gospel message to the end of the earth, including Rome. As far as Peter and the other disciples are concerned, this could have been all that Jesus meant! The newly minted Twelve (Matthias replaces Judas in 1:20–26) remain in Jerusalem, facing struggles within the holy city, but not venturing beyond its walls. It is only after the death of Stephen, the deacon who angers non-Messianic Jews by retelling Israel's story through the lens of his belief in Jesus as Messiah (7:1–60), that some disciples flee Jerusalem in 8:2. Technically 8:2 says that all people except the apostles "were scattered," but this is hyperbole since disciples clearly remained in Jerusalem (cf. Acts 11–15).

The "scattering" of these disciples amounts to the scattering of God's messengers throughout the regions of Judea and Samaria, the second level of witnessing described in Acts 1:8. Instead of following all these witnesses, however, Luke follows one: Philip (8:4). Philip travels to Samaria and "proclaimed the Messiah to them," resulting in miraculous signs, exorcisms, and joy. Given the long-standing animosity between Judeans and Samaritans, Philip's decision to travel there is surprising, as is the fact that Luke makes no mention of how surprising it is! Philip, another Spirit-filled deacon, is always the willing evangelist. Not only does he joyfully proclaim to the Samaritans, but later in the same chapter an "angel of the Lord" tells him to travel along a deserted road in southern Judea, near the coast in Gaza (8:26). Philip goes without hesitation. While on this road, he encounters the entourage of an Ethiopian official who had traveled to Jerusalem on pilgrimage, probably for Passover and Pentecost.

Although most interpreters focus on the Ethiopian official's identity as a eunuch, we should not overlook his powerful position in the story. He is a wealthy, educated, devout, and connected man. In a world where less than 5 percent of the total population could read, he sits reading his own copy of a scroll of Isaiah. He is not traveling alone, but has a chariot, as well as the people to accompany him, on his long journey to Jerusalem and back. While "Ethiopia" is an imprecise geographical location in the first century, it is considered an "end of the world" from a Roman perspective. Roman writings usually portray Ethiopians as dark skinned and tall. Romans exhibited racism and xenophobia in their writings, and often derided Ethiopians as lacking the self-control of ideal Roman men. Moreover, eunuchs were also considered to lack self-control since they were not "fully male" because they lacked testicles. In fact, several writers refer to eunuchs as "neither male nor female," language that might be familiar to those who know Paul's words in Gal 3:28. When we encounter the Ethiopian official with Philip, therefore, we encounter someone who is a paradox, according to the Roman world: this person displays elements of refined masculinity (power, wealth, servants, access, education) and uncontrolled femininity (Ethiopian, eunuch).[24] The collapsing of all these traits into a single individual in Acts drives home Luke's point: God wants everyone to hear Jesus's witnesses.

Philip does not hesitate to run up to the Ethiopian official (an action that could have aroused suspicion along a deserted road!). He also does not hesitate to speak to and teach him, even though the Ethiopian official is someone with much more power than himself. Philip shows no condescension, but only willing conversation; he does not think the Ethiopian is too powerful or too different to hear the message. The Ethiopian prompts his own baptism, and Philip, without a recorded word, baptizes him.[25] After the baptism, Philip is immediately "snatched" away by the Spirit of the Lord, but the Ethiopian official continues "on his way" (notice the double meaning here) to Ethiopia, another new witness with a message to take to the end of the earth. Although Luke does not follow the Ethiopian as he continues to travel, we should not miss the importance of this scene. Jesus's witnesses do not simply go from Jerusalem to Rome as though it were the only place God cares about. Instead, witnesses scatter everywhere, like the seeds from the Parable of the Sower. Luke may focus on the story of

Jerusalem to Rome, but he is well aware there are many others he does not trace.

Not everyone is as open to God's unlimited inclusion, however. In contrast to Philip, Peter resists acting as a witness to Gentiles. This is perhaps surprising, since he does join Phillip and John in witnessing to the Samaritans; but when God gives him a vision about "all flesh" being edible (i.e., being acceptable to God), he fights it (10:9–16). As in Luke, Peter resists three times before repenting and following the Lord's direction, this time to go to the house of a Roman centurion named Cornelius to witness (10:17–29). Peter, of course, does not think he is doing anything wrong in resisting eating unclean food, and one can hardly blame him for his skepticism in welcoming Roman soldiers. Remember, it was Rome that crucified Jesus, and centurions who nailed him to the cross. For Peter to go to a centurion's house and now say that same Jesus is resurrected and should be followed is the same as saying Rome's plan to thwart Jesus failed. Peter will be tested to confess Jesus's identity, and show his own discipleship, in the full view of a centurion instead of hiding in the courtyard (Luke 22:54–62).

Despite his initial resistance, Peter goes and witnesses on Jesus's behalf. Moreover, he is convinced of God's desire to include Gentiles when a second Pentecost-like scene takes place before his eyes (Acts 10:44–48). Even though Peter said, "I truly understand God shows no partiality, but in every nation anyone who fears him and does what is right is acceptable to him" in 10:34, it is not until 10:44–48 that he and his companions seem to comprehend it. The Holy Spirit "fell" on the gathered Gentiles without their confessing belief and regardless of age, gender, or status. The Spirit causes the Gentiles to speak "in tongues and extolling God," just as the first disciples did in 2:1–4. Peter, thus, orders for them to be baptized and even stays with them, sharing in hospitality and, therefore, friendship (see Chapter 4 on Luke). After this, Peter returns to Jerusalem and is challenged for this action, but he defends himself and Gentile inclusion, even calling *himself* (and not Paul!) the "one though whom the Gentiles would hear the message of the good news and become believers" (15:7). Although the Jerusalem believers wrestle over the presence of Gentiles, they too ultimately agree that God means to include them (15:6–41).

Acts: Disciples in the Roman Empire

The final theme I will note is the tightrope that Acts walks in its presentation of the disciples in the Roman Empire. In the Gospel, Rome is repeatedly challenged by Jesus's conception, birth, and ministry. He regularly condemns the powerful and wealthy, and Roman justice is revealed as entirely corrupt when he is killed and a centurion declares his innocence (Luke 23:47). Acts, however, seems less interested in openly condemning Rome. In fact, many interpreters have suggested that Acts presents Christians as "good Roman citizens" in Acts (cf. 1 Peter). Even though believers are persecuted, it is unjustly; they aren't actually doing anything that should cause Rome to pause. Cornelius, the Roman centurion, becomes one of the first Gentiles to join the movement, and no suggestion is made that his employment or his wealth contradicts his participation in the Way. Repeatedly, Paul (like Jesus before him) is found innocent of various false charges brought against him, and wealthy Gentiles become believers (e.g., 17:4). How do these presentations mesh with a Gospel that is so clearly opposed to wealth and a Messiah who calls on his disciples to surrender everything and follow him (Luke 14:26)?

More recent interpreters push against reading Roman accommodation and appeasement in Acts too far. After all, it is not as though Rome is presented as virtuous in Acts. Most Roman governors and bureaucrats turn a blind eye to injustice (18:16–17, 26:32), look for bribes and curry favor (24:26–27), and are more concerned with preserving themselves than the people they serve (16:35–40, 17:6–8, 22:28–29). Furthermore, the message the disciples spread is threatening to Rome: they proclaim a person executed for sedition was raised from the dead! Such a message makes Rome powerless in the face of a much more powerful God. Even though Rome claims power over the created world, for Acts, God is the one who controls events, fulfills promises, and pours out the Spirit on all flesh.

It is also important to note that while wealthy believers are presented more positively in Acts, they are not given a free pass. Instead, they are brought into the community of God's people and exist within that covenant relationship (15:22–35). While God does not require believers to relinquish their wealth, Acts highlights the believers who do so and condemns people who value money over everything else (2:42–47, 4:32–5:11, 8:18–20, 9:36–10:2, 16:16–19, 24:26). Furthermore, as a historiography, Acts is less focused on presenting an ideal life to be imitated than on the story of Jesus's message spreading in accordance with God's will. The primary life to imitate was laid out in the Gospel; in Acts, the disciples follow in Jesus's footsteps. Many times, Acts does not follow individual believers, such as Cornelius or the Ethiopian, to know what they did after repenting and joining the Way. Rather the plot keeps on moving forward, following the movement of the Spirit's witnessing through disciples all the way to Rome, while acknowledging the spread of the message is even farther.

CONCLUSIONS

Coming to the end of this chapter brings us to the end of Luke's epic two-volume story. Beginning in his Gospel, he records Jesus's life, death, and resurrection, crafting a biography meant to capture Jesus's essence and inspire Theophilus (and others) to continue in their faithful imitation of him. In Acts, the story marches forward, but not as a biography. Instead, it is a historiography, tracing one path of Jesus's disciples made Spirit-filled witnesses, wandering to different ends of the earth according to God's plan. Although this second volume is called the "Acts of the Apostles," the apostles aren't the main characters. Rather, God is the main actor in this story. In Acts, God acts primarily through the Spirit to reach disciples in various places and times. No longer limited by a human body in Jesus, this Spirit is poured out on all flesh, surprising even some of Jesus's closest followers.

Overall, Luke highlights God's control of history in both the Gospel and Acts, in spite of Roman claims to the contrary. Jesus's emphasis on God's Kingdom, inclusion of marginalized people, and willingness to sacrifice everything to fulfill God's will ultimately lead to his rejection, death, resurrection, and ascension. In Acts, these themes continue, now in the lives of the disciples who are filled with the same animating Spirit that guided Jesus in the Gospel. When the disciples give speeches in Acts, they interpret Israel's Scripture through these lenses, often sounding very similar refrains in their references to Abraham, Moses, and David (3:19–26, 7:2–53, 13:26–41). The importance of Abraham, in particular, brings Luke's story full circle. For Luke, God had always planned to include the Gentiles, and Jesus is the means of doing so. This does not relegate the Jews to a lesser place in God's story, but to a primary place because of Jesus's Jewish identity (e.g., Luke 1–2). The stretch to include others in Jesus's ministry continues in the incorporation of Samaritans, Ethiopians, Diaspora Jews, and Gentiles of all kinds in Acts. God's continuing to surprise and teach the disciples in Acts can be read as encouraging Theophilus, and other Christians, to continue being open to God's Spirit as well by seeing God's love for all people, regardless of how "different" they (or we) may perceive them to be.

John's Story

Recognizing the Incarnate Word

THE FINAL GOSPEL IN THE NT is the Gospel of John. While it
retells the life story of the same Jesus of Nazareth as the Synoptic
Gospels, its version is different. Often called the "spiritual" Gospel,
John uses symbolism, double meanings, and a unique description of Jesus as the Word of God become flesh (1:1, 14). Although
for most of Christian history interpreters thought John used the
Synoptic Gospels, there was a stretch of time in the twentieth century that many scholars believed John offered an independent version of the Jesus story. With renewed interest in the topic, however,
more scholars are returning to the older view.[1] John, like Luke,
seems to have known other Gospel accounts. John's Gospel not only
preserves elements from the Synoptic tradition, but also challenges
them with an unwavering and undoubtedly divine Jesus.

In this chapter, we will explore John's unique version of the
Jesus story, paying special attention to the way this Gospel focuses
on the theme of recognition.[2] While this theme is a part of the
Synoptic accounts, they also give significant attention to Jesus's
message about the Kingdom of God. In John's Gospel, however,
understanding Jesus's message is collapsed with understanding
Jesus's identity. Special emphasis is placed on believing in Jesus's
name (1:12–13, 3:14–18) and knowing he is "the Christ, the Son
of God" to receive eternal life (20:30–31). While Jesus's kingship
emerges a couple times in John, the focus is on his embodiment
of God's will on earth and the challenge people in the world face

An Introduction to the Gospels and Acts. Alicia D. Myers, Oxford University Press. © Oxford University
Press 2022. DOI: 10.1093/oso/9780190926809.003.0006

recognizing him. Integrating Israel's Scripture, John claims Jesus's coming is consistent with, and decipherable from, a close reading of Israel's story (5:39–47). Informed by rhetoric, philosophy, and even classical drama, the Gospel of John argues only those who recognize Jesus can understand this truth.

CONTEXTUALIZING THE COMPOSITION

According to tradition, the Gospel and Letters of John (1, 2, and 3 John) were composed in Ephesus sometime between 90 and 110 CE. This makes John's Gospel the last to be written among the four found in the NT. Written after the destruction of the Jerusalem temple, John's Gospel emerges during reigns of either Domitian (r. 91–96 CE), Nerva (r. 96–98 CE), or Trajan (r. 98–117 CE). Emperor Trajan's correspondence with Pliny the Younger, governor of the province of Bithynia (modern-day Turkey), just to the northeast of Ephesus, around 112 CE shows conflict between Rome and Christians who placed their allegiance to Jesus's kingship over that of the emperor.[3] Although we should not connect these letters to the Gospel of John directly, their existence points to tension believers in the region could have faced.

The traditional figure behind these works is John the son of Zebedee. The Gospel of John is like the other canonical Gospels, though, in maintaining authorial anonymity: John is nowhere named as the author. Instead, the authority behind this story is the Beloved Disciple, so called because of Jesus's specific love mentioned in 13:23, 19:26, and 21:20. Tradition identifies this disciple as John, son of Zebedee, but there are several problems with this conclusion. First, this John is consistently associated with his brother, James, in the Synoptic Gospels, but James does not appear explicitly in John. Moreover, the Beloved Disciple seems to be from Jerusalem and, thus, "known to the high priest" (18:15). It is hard to imagine, although not impossible, that a fisherman from Galilee had such connections. Instead of John of Zebedee, interpreters have suggested Lazarus, whom Jesus is said to "love" (11:3, 36; cf. 20:2), and even Mary Magdalene, as possibilities. Yet the Gospel goes to lengths to retain the Beloved Disciple's anonymity, even if he (or she) were known to the original audiences. Reading the Gospel now, we are left with a mystery, but I will refer to the author as "John" for ease of reference.[4]

The historical situations that may have prompted the Gospel's composition have also received a lot of scholarly attention over the years, not least because of the Gospel's harsh polemic against "the Jews," who appear as a group character within it, repeatedly opposing Jesus. Attempting to solve this issue in the wake of the Holocaust, J. Louis Martyn surmised a schism in the background of the Gospel of John.[5] Martyn theorized a developing Christian community kicked out of local Jewish synagogues due to their belief in Jesus's divinity. This, for Martyn, explained the animosity toward the Jews in John. Other scholars, however, suggest we should not assume Jews did (or could) excommunicate individuals from local synagogues; Johannine Christians may have left of their own accord.[6] At present scholars are wary of trying to reconstruct the history of a "Johannine community" too precisely. Most still conclude the Gospel points to some sort of conflict between Jesus's disciples and other Jews, but others suggest the Gospel itself might be responsible for instigating conflict and even creating the community it describes.[7] Either way, the Gospel encourages its audience to remain faithful as God's elected few who recognize Jesus while the world rejected him (6:45–46, 15:18–25).

The importance of rightly recognizing Jesus is reflected in his words and actions throughout the Gospel, which differ significantly from the Synoptics. Jesus does not perform exorcisms and rarely speaks in parables or about the Kingdom of God. Instead, he performs "signs" (*semeia*, 2:11, 4:54, 20:30) followed by lengthy speeches explaining his unique identity as God's Son (e.g., 5:18–47). Jesus's speeches use classical rhetorical techniques and structures, perhaps another indication of the author's education and situation. As the latest canonical Gospel written, John communicates a late first- or early second-century situation for early Christians outside of Palestine. Increasingly separated from Jewish contexts, believers in this time faced increased suspicion from nonbelieving Jews and Gentiles, as well as Roman officials. While these circumstances might explain, they do not excuse the harsh polemic against the Jews in John. We should also note that Rome is characterized as unjust and violent in John. Indeed, Rome's tendency to massacre motivates the high priest's decision to condemn Jesus in John 11. Written after the devastation of Jerusalem, Caiaphas's words about fearing Roman destruction of the temple and the people acknowledge a known reality.[8] John's Gospel does not ignore Rome's violence, but it does argue that the reward for following Jesus is worth the risk.

Digging Deeper: Hellenistic Philosophies and the Search for Truth

John's Gospel emphasizes the difficulty of recognizing Jesus, both during his lifetime and in its aftermath. Rather than singling out the Jews, the whole world is alienated from its Creator in John, making recognition of life and light impossible without divine assistance. Recognition is a common feature of Greco-Roman literature, especially in classical drama. "Recognition" (*anagnōrisis*) scenes convey the difficulty of discerning truth, and the emotional heft we experience with a sudden reversal of fortunes. The drama, or trauma, of sudden recognition can lead to relief and joy or shock and dismay. For Aristotle, that made recognition scenes a key feature in successful tragedies, but they also appear in a wide variety of ancient genres.[9]

The recognition of truth, or authentic knowledge, was also the focus of philosophical schools in the Hellenistic world.[10] Platonic thinkers sought truth or "the Good" beyond the physical world, while those more influenced by Aristotle sought to access that truth through observing the physical world. Neopythagoreans traced their lineage to the famed mathematician and philosopher, Pythagoras, but like Platonists sought truth beyond the material world, often through mathematical means. These schools of thought would eventually merge in the later second century CE and beyond to form what scholars now call "Neoplatonism," which dominated the philosophical landscape of late antiquity.

Other popular philosophical schools of the first and second centuries CE included Stoicism and Epicureanism. Founded by Xeno of Citium (ca. 344–262 BCE), Stoicism sought to understand the order of the cosmos and fate in order to determine what was truly valuable and what was not. Stoicism became increasingly popular throughout the Hellenistic period and among influential Romans, including Seneca (ca. 4 BCE–65 CE) and Emperor Marcus Aurelius (ca. 121–180 CE). Rather than being emotionless, Stoics sought to understand their place in the cosmos in order to avoid the sorrow caused by the futile resistance of one's fate. Like the modern-day "serenity prayer," Stoics focused on what they could change and learned to accept the things they couldn't.[11] Epicureans, too, sought to avoid extremes in order to find happiness free from physical or mental stressors. Founded by Epicurus (ca. 341–270 BCE), Epicureanism differed from many philosophies by rejecting the idea of an immaterial "Good." Instead, Epicurus focused on the material world and did not believe there was an afterlife. Although they have garnered a reputation for hedonism in contemporary times, Epicureans avoided extreme pleasure, just as they avoided extreme pain. They sought a middle ground and argued fear of death and fear of the gods were meaningless since, on the one hand, death is unavoidable and, on the other, the gods do not interfere with human lives.

Outlining these basic features of major Hellenistic philosophies reveals their consistent focus on truth and the peace, even happiness, it brings for those who recognize it. As with the

Jewish schools of thought we explored in Chapter 3, most people didn't have time to participate in these debates, but their influence permeated society and reflected the underlying assumption that the cosmos is grounded in order. Order, rather than chaos, was "wisdom" (*sophia*), the very thing *philosophy* was named to "love" (*philos*). Jewish groups, too, assumed God's creation of life as a type of ordering, with Wisdom personified as God's helper in Proverbs 8 and Sirach 24. Wisdom, sometimes aligned with the Torah, showed all those who come to her how to follow God's orderly will.

The assumption of order, or wisdom, at the core of all life meant a philosopher's goal was to decipher that order. Jewish authors and philosophers likewise sought to show how following God's will meant living according to the ways of Wisdom. This common focus encouraged some Jewish philosophers, such as Philo of Alexandria, to combine Jewish ideas with Hellenistic philosophies in hopes of showing the value of Jewish practices and beliefs. In Roman contexts, some non-Jews expressed an appreciation of Jewish practices because of the emphasis on self-control shown in sabbaths, fast days, and dietary laws. Non-Jews participated in synagogues and Jewish practices without becoming full proselytes through circumcision or even necessarily limiting their belief to the God of Israel alone. Contemporary scholars refer to these people as "God-fearers."[12] Some evidence for non-Jewish participants at synagogues comes from Acts' presentation of Paul's preaching at synagogues throughout the Diaspora, as well as Cornelius's support for the synagogue in Caesarea (Acts 10).

Who Is Jesus? Paradox, Irony, and Recognition in the Gospel of John

The Gospel of John joins in this larger world of truth-seeking with its own version of needed recognition. Set in a Jewish worldview, John uses Israel's Scriptures as the backdrop for its story of Jesus, who is God's Word (or Wisdom) come in flesh to the world it helped to create (1:1–5). Consistent with philosophical assumptions, the

Word is originally outside of and beyond the created order; it must come down into the cosmos ("the world") to bring truth to people who cannot otherwise access it. The Gospel of John, therefore, reflects the philosophical assumptions of its context and uses recognition-type scenes to narrate Jesus's mission. As mentioned above, these scenes are common in Greco-Roman literature, especially dramas. Perhaps the most famous of these scenes is from Sophocles's *Oedipus Rex*, when Oedipus recognizes his real identity and blinds himself when he learns he married his mother! In these scenes, two characters meet and come to recognize one another, resulting in either joy or tragedy. Recognition can happen through the use of tokens (physical scars or appearances), memory, logical inference, or poetic contrivance (where the author just makes the recognition happen without explanation).[13] A variety of these scenes happen in John's Gospel alongside repeated misrecognitions, fueling the plot as it moves toward Jesus's death and resurrection.

Jesus is the incarnate Word of Life in the Gospel of John. He is human-born, having a mother, father, and siblings (2:1–12, 6:42, 7:1–5, 19:25–27), but he is also the "Unique One" (*monogenēs*) and "God" (1:18, 3:18, 20:28), containing within himself a paradox of temporal existence and eternal being.[14] As a walking paradox, Jesus acts in keeping with his identity as the Word become flesh rather than his physical appearance: he looks like a Galilean Jewish man, less than fifty years of age (2:18–20, 8:40–58). While some know his physical parentage, Jesus has no known education that would justify his teaching ability or authority (1:45, 6:42, 7:15). Despite these facts, Jesus speaks with rhetorical nuance, shows his understanding of Israel's Scriptures, and provides life to those who trust him even as he faces increasing hostility from those whom he baffles. Rather than adapting to help humans understand him, the Johannine Jesus repeatedly increases the confusion around him, saying that doing otherwise would be lying (8:55). Jesus's behavior eventually sparks violence. Not a hapless victim, Jesus orchestrates his mission from beginning to end in order to return to the Father and send the Holy Spirit in his place. The Spirit, unlimited by a physical body, brings truth to an ever-greater number of those who recognize Jesus (John 14–17).

Readers of John's Gospel regularly highlight philosophical connections between Jesus, his message, and Stoic or Platonic philosophies of the era. Some note similarities in this Gospel's use of Scripture and characterization of Jesus as God's Word with the work of the Jewish philosopher Philo of Alexandria.[15] Philo was a prolific author whose allegorical interpretations of Scripture reflect Stoic and Platonic ideas from his milieu. Others connect John's story more closely with Platonism or Stoicism, suggesting this Gospel takes a philosophical approach to Jesus's story with its language of light, *logos* (word), and spirit (*pneuma*).[16] Rather than selecting just one of these philosophies as the lens through which to read John, however, it seems better to view John as a product of its own culture, which was permeated with ideas of seeking truth that was somehow beyond the physical world. Living a life connected to truth was believed to bring an inner peace, but not always an actual physical peace, as the life of Socrates or Jesus demonstrates.

In John's Gospel, Jesus traverses the divide between the immaterial and material by means of his incarnation, resulting in his paradoxical existence. Moreover, although the world was made by and through God's Word, creation cannot recognize this Word when it visits the world in the flesh (1:1–11). According to John's metaphors, the world exists in darkness because people care more about earning glory from one another than they do about glorifying God (5:39–47). Humans are fickle and fearful (2:23–25, 8:30–33, 10:19–21). They are drawn to displays of material power—such as Jesus's visible signs—but they are also afraid; those in power fear losing their power, and everyone fears those who they think have more power than themselves. When Jesus confronts Jewish religious and political leaders, they react harshly against him, challenging Jesus to prove his identity and verify his claims (5:16–18, 8:12–30). Rather than focusing on God's power, these leaders fear

Rome, whose ability to quell any perceived rebellion with rapid and complete violence sparks the final plot to arrest Jesus in John 11.

The harsh characterizations of Jewish religious and political leaders lead many to read the Gospel of John as an anti-Jewish story.[17] The use of this Gospel by anti-Semitic groups in the past, as well as undergirding anti-Jewish sentiment in contemporary contexts, warrants caution. From the perspective of the late first century, however, it might be anachronistic to consider John anti-Jewish, especially given the fact that Jesus-followers were still largely seen as Jews themselves. In this vein, John represents another facet of intra-Jewish debates, rather than opposing Jewish practices, beliefs, or ethnicity. Salvation remains "from the Jews" in John (4:22), and Israel's Scriptures remain authoritative, but both these ideas are interpreted through John's particular lens of Jesus's identity and mission as God's Word incarnate.

We should also remember most of John's audiences were likely already Jesus-believers, though evangelistic aims should not be ignored (20:30–31).[18] John's Gospel encourages believers to see that they have access to the Holy Spirit, who reveals Jesus's identity to them regardless of human opposition (14:15–31, 15:26–16:15). For John, it is not surprising that the world, and especially those in power, did not recognize Jesus in their midst or after his resurrection. As in other Jewish writings about Wisdom, and Hellenistic philosophies that contemplate "the Good," God's ways are inscrutable to humans without divine assistance. Yet, in John, neither Jesus nor the Father is undone by the world's blindness. Instead, Jesus's rejection is part of God's larger plan to make the Spirit of truth available to more people (16:8–13, 17:1–26). As the Gospel of John ends, Jesus offers a blessing for those "who believed but did not see" him in the flesh (20:29). Rather than missing out, those who came to believe after Jesus's life, death, and resurrection are *blessed* because of their access to the Spirit who teaches them how to understand Jesus. If they had met him in their own lives, the Gospel implies, they too would have been confounded and probably also among his rejectors.

LITERARY OVERVIEW

Reading John as the final of the four canonical accounts, we cannot help but compare it to the Synoptic Gospels. While past scholars focused on Johannine independence, recent scholarship explores possible connections to Synoptic traditions, especially from Mark and Luke. One of the most apparent examples is in John 12 and Mark 14, which narrate Jesus's reaction to his upcoming death. In Mark 14, Jesus breaks down in sorrow: "And going a little farther, he threw himself on the ground and prayed that, if it were possible, the hour might pass from him" (v. 35). John's Jesus directly refutes this characterization in 12:27–28, saying, "Now my soul is troubled. And what shall I say—'Father save me from this hour?' No, it is for this reason that I have come to this hour." John's Jesus does not deny the emotion, but he refutes any hint of hesitation. Unlike the more human Jesus in Mark, John's Jesus is fully aware of his mission in the Gospel of John. He unswervingly suffers and dies to show his love for his disciples, whom he calls "friends" and "siblings" (*philoi*, 15:15; *adelphoi*, 20:17), so that they might imitate this love in caring for one another (13:34–35, 15:12–14).

The different characterization of Jesus in John, with its heavy emphasis on his paradoxical identity as both divine and human, also leads to a rearrangement of Jesus's story in this biography. The story retains recognizable elements from the Synoptic accounts—Jesus heals, walks on water, feeds a multitude, teaches, clears out the temple, dies, and is resurrected—but not without alteration. John's Jesus does not perform exorcisms, and he uses parables in a more limited sense, often integrating them into a speech (3:5–8, 4:34–38, 5:19–20, 10:1–18, 16:21–22).[19] John also moves Jesus's temple scene from just before his death to the beginning of the Gospel, at the first of three Passover festivals (2:13–25).[20] Jesus's temple outburst sets the stage for his public ministry rather than its climactic conclusion. It anticipates the continued conflicts he has with Jewish leaders and contributes to the larger motif of Jesus's body as a new temple (2:20–22). As the "dwelling place" (or sanctuary, *skēnoō*) where God's Word resides (1:14–16; Exodus 33–34), Jesus is the location of God's presence on earth. He hints at this identity with his disciples in John 1:51 as well as with the Samaritan woman in 4:19–24. When the people come to Jesus rather than the temple before the third, and final, Passover in John, the conflict begun in John 2 comes full circle (12:9).

Most outlines break John's Gospel into two main parts—the Book of Signs (1:19–12:51) and the Book of Glory (3:1–20:31)—plus a prologue (1:1–18) and epilogue (21:1–25). There are reasons to commend this outline, not least because Jesus summarizes his public ministry in chapter 12 and notes the arrival of his "hour" (i.e., his death) in 13:1–3. While not dismissing this popular outline, the one below highlights the pervasiveness of the Jewish liturgical calendar in John. I have also incorporated both the prologue (1:1–18) and epilogue (21:1–25) since we have no evidence the Gospel was ever transmitted without these portions.

Introducing the Word (1:1–51)
  First words (1:1–5)
  Coming into the world (1:6–14)
  From John to Jesus (1:15–51)

Beginning Jesus's ministry (2:1–5:1)
  The first sign and first Passover (2:1–3:21)
  John's continued witness (3:22–4:3)
  Samaria and the second sign (4:4–5:1)

Festivals and confusion (5:1–10:39)
  Sabbath in Jerusalem (5:2–47)
  The second Passover (6:1–71)
  Tabernacles and a second sabbath in Jerusalem (7:1–10:21)
  Feast of Dedication (10:22–42)

Transition toward the "hour" (11:1–17:26)
    Resurrection, life, and fear of death (11:1–12:11)
    The hour arrives: the third Passover (12:12–13:30)
    Jesus's consolation and commands (13:31–17:26)

Returning to the Father (18:1–21:25)
    Jesus lays down his life (18:1–19:42)
    New beginnings: resurrection and commission
       (20:1–21:25)

Looking through this outline, it is clear John does not narrate as many miracles as in the Synoptics, even though Jesus's ministry is two years longer. John, however, indicates there was great care taken in the selection of events told, explaining:

> Now Jesus did many other signs before his disciples that have not been written in this book. But these have been written so that you might believe that Jesus is the Christ the Son of God, and by believing you might have life in his name. (20:30–31, my translation)

These verses are considered the thesis of John's Gospel. The careful selection of events is also evident in the use of the Jewish liturgical calendar; the festivals and their OT backgrounds provide insight into Jesus's actions and the conflicts they engender.

Additional literary features of John's Gospel include Jesus's frequent "I am" statements; his lengthy speeches; the use of symbolism; and the date of Jesus's death on the Day of Preparation for Passover. Jesus emphasizes the solemnness of his words with the refrain, "Amen, amen, I am saying to you" and he punctuates his teaching with "I am" statements. Sometimes the "I am" sayings associate Jesus with another image; the symbolism is often rooted in OT and Second Temple Judaism.[21] Interestingly, Jesus repeatedly compares himself to things rather than specific people: bread of life, light of the world, gate, good shepherd, resurrection and life, the truth, vine, and so on. Other times Jesus leaves the "I am" statement without a predicate noun to complete the phrase (4:26, 6:20, 13:19, 18:5–6, 8). Most scholars connect these statements to God's name as "I am who I am" from Exod 3:14, once again reinforcing Jesus's connection to God, whom he calls "Father." These "I am" statements, and Jesus's lengthy speeches, also present a shift in the content of Jesus's message in John. Whereas in the Synoptics, Jesus spends much time discussing the Kingdom of God, in John, Jesus focuses his message on his identity and the life that recognizing him brings. For John, access to God's Kingdom (or "eternal life") only comes by trusting its King.

KEY PASSAGES AND THEMES

In the Beginning: John's Opening Words

Rather than a birth narrative like Luke, or a genealogy like Matthew, John begins with a poetic prologue. The prologue is commonly considered to include all of John 1:1–18, but this is a rather recent definition (ca. 1777). The prologue is broken up in several places, most notably the interruptions describing the witnessing ministry of John (whom the Synoptics call "the Baptist") in verses 6–9 and 15–16 (or 18).[22] Perhaps reflecting these interruptions, earlier interpreters divided the prologue differently, some manuscripts separating 1:1–5 from what follows, while others put a break after 1:14. Interpreters like Augustine of Hippo (ca. 354–430 CE) ended the prologue with the Word's "becoming flesh" (*sarx egeneto*) in 1:14, which forms an *inclusio* with the description of creation having "become" (*egeneto*) because of the Word in 1:1–3.[23] More recent interpreters stretch the prologue to verse 18, often finding a chiasm that pivots on the authority of those who received the Word to "become children of God" (1:12–13).[24] Regardless of the precise divisions of the prologue, however, readers throughout history have noted its unique role in setting up the remainder of the Gospel story.

In a manner similar to the prologues proceeding Greek dramas, John's prologue highlights major characters, plot events, and themes that surface in the rest of the story, elevating the events to a cosmic level to emphasize their importance.[25] In John 1:1–5 we learn the "Word" (*logos*) has no beginning, but rather was "with God" and "was God" from time eternal. This scene recreates the narrative of Genesis 1, reminding the audience of God's speaking that caused light and life. In John, this same light and life-giving Word "is coming into the world," heralded by the messenger named "John" (1:6–9). This John is not the traditional Gospel author, but John the Baptist. Although important, John is dwarfed by the Word about whom he witnesses. In 1:10–11, we find out the Word is coming into the cosmos it helped create and sustains, but creation does not recognize it. Those who do recognize it, however, "are given authority to become children of God" (1:12). In 1:13 the Gospel uses striking language of begetting with Aristotelian overtones about pregnancy and childbirth that portrays the "word" or "order" (*logos*) provided by male semen giving shape to the child born.[26] In John's view, God's ultimate Word coming into the world recreates those who accept it, so that they are born anew as God's children (cf. John 1:13, 3:1–8, 20:22).

In 1:14, we learn that God's Word "became flesh," moving from the realm of eternal "being" (*eimi*) to the created order that is "becoming" (*ginomai*). The Word "dwelled" (*eskēnōsen*) among the "us" of the Gospel, mirroring the glory of God living among the wandering Israelites in the traveling Tabernacle (*skēnē*). Like the Tabernacle, the incarnate Word is also the location and revelation of God's glory. In 1:15–16, John's witness again bursts into the scene, confirming his subordinate status to the one who comes after him since this one was before him. Finally, 1:17–18 compares Moses and the Torah ("law," *nomos*) to Jesus and the "grace and truth" that "becomes" (or "happens") through him. Jesus does not compete with Moses; rather his work is coherent alongside that of

Moses (cf. 3:14, 5:45–47). Jesus is nevertheless superior to Moses; while Moses shares that which he was "given," Jesus enables the "becoming" of grace and truth in ways that resonate with the Word's creative activity in 1:1–5. Verse 18 returns to the divine language of 1:1 again, explicitly calling Jesus "unique God" (*monogenēs theos*) and the one "who is in the bosom of the Father" (my translation). The Gospel narrative follows this sequence: having become flesh, God's creative Word comes, is rejected by most and accepted by a few, and then returns to the Father's bosom from which he came.

John's prologue forms the basis for all the irony that follows. The Gospel audience alone hears the prologue; no other character, not even John the Baptist, has such a complete explanation of Jesus's mission and divinity. Although the narrative characters meet Jesus in the flesh, he routinely confuses and confounds them with his words and actions. His works and words are meant to be testimony to prove his unique identity, but most characters in John's Gospel are confused and reject the Life who stands before them because they are accustomed to the darkness of the world (1:10–11, 3:18–21). John's irony contributes to the Gospel's rhetorical goals to (1) emphasize Jesus's unique identity as God's Son and Christ and (2) highlight the "blessed" status of those who didn't meet him in person. Perhaps discouraged because they never saw their Savior, John's Gospel casts its audience as blessed by having access both to the Holy Spirit and the Gospel itself, which gives them a more complete portrait of Jesus (20:29).

Jesus's Speeches and Signs

Although he is the Word "become flesh," Jesus was born and *looks* just like any other person in the Gospel of John. In fact, it is the contrast between his physical appearance, and the expectations it creates, with his words and actions that provides fuel for Gospel's plot. In John, Jesus performs a "work" or a "sign" and follows it with speeches explaining how his identity is revealed and confirmed by that sign. The speeches are sometimes dialogues, but Jesus regularly outspeaks his companions, and early episodes often end without a clear conclusion made by other narrative characters. As the conflict ratchets up in chapters 6 and following, most characters either reject or remain unsure of Jesus. As in the other Gospels, he is betrayed by Judas, one of the Twelve, and denied by Peter. Yet, in John, Jesus clearly knows of these upcoming events, prophesying them ahead of time to engender belief (6:70–71, 13:18–19, 36–38). Moreover, he is not alone on the cross. His mother is present with other women, and the anonymous Beloved Disciple, who receive his instructions before Jesus chooses the moment of his death (19:25–30).

In Jesus's first defensive speech of the Gospel, John 5:19–47, he argues his works are among the witnesses to his identity as God's Son. In fact, Jesus lists four types of witnesses in this speech, all of which fit categories from classical rhetoric and are illustrated in Table 6.1.

The most compelling types of witness were ancient and divine, thus making Jesus's appeal to God as his Father the most significant witness in his list.[27] The testifying function of Jesus's works explains why this Gospel also calls them "signs," since they point to the deeper revelation of his identity. Signs also further the connection between Jesus and Moses, who performed signs to convince the Israelites and Egyptians of God's deliverance (Exod 4:17, 28).

In John 5, Jesus's work gained the ire of the Jewish religious leaders not because he healed a man, but because he did so *on the*

Table 6.1

TESTIMONY IN JOHN 5

Type of testimony	Human	Divine
Ancient	Moses and Scripture (5:39–47)	Father (5:37)
Recent	John "the Baptist" (5:33–35)	Jesus's works (5:36)

sabbath (5:9–16). Rather than denying his role, Jesus confronts the leaders and justifies his actions by claiming a unique relationship to God, whom he calls his own Father (5:17–18). Jesus argues since his Father is working on the sabbath, he also works, just as a son imitates his father by learning his trade (5:19–20). The commonplace comparison to a regular father and son intensifies the audacity of Jesus's claim. Jesus may look like a regular man, but he is anything from normal. He doesn't imitate a human father, but God alone who has given him "life in himself" and "judgment" so that he might receive the same honor God receives (5:21–29). "I can do nothing on my own," Jesus says. "I seek to do not my own will but the will of him who sent me" (5:30).

Jesus's later works and speeches reinforce the themes introduced in John 5 and likewise fit the initial presentation of Jesus as the Word become flesh from the prologue. The healing miracle from 5:1–18 is still being debated by the religious leaders in John 7–8 when Jesus arrives secretly to participate in the Festival of Tabernacles. Once again, Jesus does not shy away from the controversy but engages the divided crowd and antagonistic leaders before healing again on another sabbath in John 9 when he gives sight to a man born blind. The conflict continues to build in John 9–10 when Jesus compares the religious leaders to cowardly shepherds, and even thieves and wolves, who sacrifice their sheep rather than protecting them. Jesus's actions and speeches are consistent, but their consistency intensifies the conflict. This pattern reinforces the Gospel's point: the *real* challenge is recognizing Jesus's identity.

Recognitions and Mistakes: Other Characters

Jesus meets with a variety of characters during his ministry in John's Gospel. These characters differ in gender, socioeconomic and political status, prestige, and ethnicity. The majority of the characters are "crowds" of Jews, or Judeans. As I noted in Chapter 3, the term "Jew/Judean" (*Ioudaios*) refers people from the Roman province of Judea, or those whose ancestors are from Judea. In Palestine itself, Judea also refers to the southern portion near Jerusalem (see Figure 3.1 in Chapter 3). Jesus himself is a Jew (or Judean), being from the province of Judea and descended from Judeans. He is also a Galilean, meaning he comes from the northern and more rural part of Palestine rather than the southern and more urban area near Jerusalem. Jesus spends most of his time with other Jewish characters: the first disciples whom he collects are from Galilee, but others live near Jerusalem, such as the family of Mary, Martha, and Lazarus (11:1–12:8). Still other characters are Samaritans, who welcome Jesus into their midst after receiving the testimony of the Samaritan woman (4:1–42). In 4:43–54, Jesus is in Galilee when he meets a "royal official" (*basilikos*), presumably from Herod Antipas's household, and heals his son with words alone. While "Greeks" (*Hellēnes*) ask to see Jesus in 12:20 and Jesus converses with Pilate during his trial, Jesus's focus remains on Jews throughout this Gospel.

Jesus repeatedly engages individual characters who come to him apart from crowds. These characters often fair better than the divisive crowds as they listen to Jesus one on one. The scene with the Samaritan woman, for example, reframes the OT type-scene of hospitality and betrothal beside a well (4:1–26; cf. Gen 24:10–67, 29:10–20). Rather than negotiating for marriage, Jesus and the woman have a deeply theological conversation that leads to her sharing news of Jesus's arrival in her town, overcoming the historical divide between Jews and Samaritans (Figure 6.1).

Other women, too, have important roles such as Jesus's mother, who initiates his public ministry in 2:1–12 and is present for its close as he hangs on the cross in 19:25–30. Martha and Mary are more prominent than their resurrected brother, Lazarus. Martha offers the most complete confession of Jesus's identity in 11:27, and Mary anoints Jesus for his burial in 12:1–8. Finally, Mary Magdalene becomes the first apostle when she is sent by Jesus to share the news of his resurrection with the disciples after experiencing a reunion in the garden (20:10–18).

FIGURE 6.1 *Christ and the Samaritan by the Well*, by Angelika Kauffman. 1796. Oil on canvas. Bavarian State Painting Collections. Public Domain. Wikimedia Commons.

These women, along with other characters who recognize Jesus, have a consistent trait: they don't have much power in the current social system. They will not lose power if the system changes, nor are they responsible for anyone who relies on them for protection. On the one hand, this lack of attachment to the world's system frees these characters to receive what the Gospel presents as divine revelation. On the other hand, their recognition of Jesus puts them in precarious positions with those who are in power, perhaps making them visible to authorities for the first time. Thus, after benefiting from Jesus's miraculous intervention, the man born blind is cast out from his community, and the chief priests also plot to put the recently resurrected Lazarus to death (9:34–38, 12:9–11). By associating with Jesus, these characters cast their lot with him, for better or worse. The Gospel, therefore, seeks to convince believers that the sacrifice is worth it. The world might hate them, but such hatred is meaningless in contrast to the love and life they receive as God's children (15:18–25).

As in the Synoptic accounts, people in power regularly struggle with and reject Jesus in John. Only three characters from the ruling class come to Jesus: Nicodemus (3:1–21, 7:45–52, 19:38–42), the royal official (4:46–54), and Joseph of Arimathea (19:38–42). John suggests there are other leaders who believe, but they remain in secret because they fear being "put out of the synagogue" (12:42–43). Yet there are more risks for those in power if they align themselves with Jesus. As Caiaphas and the other Jerusalem leaders note, they risk Rome's violence against "the place" (i.e., the temple) and the people they are supposed to protect (11:48). From their vantage point, these leaders are being good shepherds by focusing Rome's gaze on Jesus because "it is better for one man to die for the people than to have the whole nation destroyed" (11:50). The narrator interprets Caiaphas's words as prophetic: Jesus will die for the nation, "and not for the nation only, but to gather into one [*synagogē eis hen*] the dispersed children of God" (11:52). The people in power are afraid because of Jesus, but they fear Rome rather than the God Jesus reveals. Instead of a defeat, however, the Gospel argues that Jesus's death is the means of their reunification—their "in gathering" (*synagogē*)—to create a new synagogue connected to one another and to God (17:1–26).

Returning to the Father: Jesus's Death and Resurrection

The plot of John's Gospel shifts toward Jesus's death in chapter 11. Jesus's final trip to Jerusalem before his death is during the Feast of Dedication (or Hanukkah). This festival celebrates the rededication of the temple to God alone after the successful ouster of Antiochus IV Epiphanes and his images of Zeus in 164 BCE (see Chapter 2). The focus of Dedication is on God's oneness and sole worth of worship, as is emphasized in the Shema from Deut

6:4: "Hear, O Israel, the Lord your God, the Lord is One." During this festival, Jesus makes the audacious claim in John 10:30, "I and the Father are One," thus prompting the crowd to try to stone him in 10:31 and ushering him out of Jerusalem for the last time before his passion begins.

In John 11, Jesus returns to Judea to raise his "friend" (*philos*, 11:11) Lazarus from the dead as his last public sign. As before, it causes division among those who see it. Some believe, but others report the event to the Jerusalem leaders, who "gather together" (*synagogon*) and decide to arrange Jesus's death, as discussed above (11:45–54). When Jesus is anointed by Lazarus's sister, Mary, in 12:1–8 Jesus interprets the event as preparing his body for burial, and when he enters Jerusalem in 12:12, it is for the last time. He gives his final public address in 12:20–36 to a crowd of Jews and Greeks who have gathered for Passover. The mixed crowd is often tied to Isaiah's promise of Gentiles coming to Jerusalem in the eschaton, reinforcing the end of Jesus's ministry in John. Jesus, then, predicts his death again before the narrator explains his rejection by citing Isa 6:10, the same passage used for this purpose in the Synoptics and Acts (Mark 4:12; Matt 13:14–15; Luke 8:10; Acts 28:26–27).

After Jesus utters a summary of his public ministry in 12:44–50, the Gospel shifts to final preparations for his death. He retreats to spend private time with his disciples in John 13–17, having a last meal where he washes their feet instead of giving them bread and wine, as he does in the Synoptics. For John, the emphasis is on imitating Jesus's self-sacrificing actions, symbolized in the washing of feet, but ultimately displayed by his dying on the cross. After Judas's departure into the ominous darkness of night, Jesus offers his longest speech of the Gospel in 13:31–17:26. Uninterrupted by the narrator, Jesus speaks to his disciples in the Gospel as well as to those listening or reading the Gospel, comforting and encouraging them with the argument that he is returning to his Father. Unlike the Synoptics, it is the disciples who need comforting before Jesus's arrest, rather than Jesus himself. "I will not leave you orphaned,"

Jesus promises. "I am coming to you" (14:18). Moreover, Jesus's departure means he will "ask the Father, and he will give you another Advocate [*Paraclete*] to be with you forever" (14:15). This second Advocate is the Holy Spirit, who will continue Jesus's ministry by "teach[ing] you everything and remind[ing] you of all that I have said to you" (14:26). In John's Gospel, it is better that Jesus leaves the disciples so that the Spirit can come. Unlimited by space or time, the Spirit enlivens the disciples forever.

Jesus's command of events continues through his arrest, trials, and death in John 18–19. Even while on the cross, Jesus knows what must take place. He knowingly fulfills Scripture by asking for a drink, while the soldiers and those around him ignorantly play their parts in God's plan. The contrast of Jesus's knowledge versus the characters' obliviousness is a constant feature of John's Gospel, but it reaches a fever pitch in John 13–19. Jesus is implacable in the face of a horrible and humiliating death even as those around him claim a false victory. When Jesus dies, it is not with a cry of being forsaken, but a triumphant, "It is finished!" before he "bowed his head and gave up his spirit" (19:30). Dying at the same time the Passover lambs were traditionally slaughtered, John's Jesus is the "Lamb of God" who signifies God's deliverance of Israel, even though he remains unrecognized (1:29, 36, 19:36).

Jesus won't be recognized immediately, even after his resurrection in John 20. In this chapter, John artfully places two recognition scenes side by side: first, with Mary Magdalene, who stands abandoned by Peter and the Beloved Disciple near Jesus's empty tomb (20:10–18); and second, with Thomas, who craves further proof to trust Jesus's message (20:24–29). Mary's garden scene with Jesus is perhaps the clearest recognition scene of the Gospel, since she first mistakes Jesus for the gardener. She recognizes him only once he says her name, "Miriam!" to which she responds, "Rabboni" ("My teacher," 20:16; cf. 1:38, 49, 3:2, 26, 4:31, 6:25, 9:2, 11:8). This exchange fulfills Jesus's promise that he knows the names of those who are his, and that they recognize his voice (10:3, 16, 27). Thomas's scene is a bit different. Rather than sorrow, Jesus combats

Thomas's incredulity and perhaps anger. Thomas recognizes Jesus's physical appearance not when Jesus says his name, but when Jesus shows Thomas the scars from his injuries suffered on the cross (20:25, 27). These are the tokens, or signs, that Jesus is truly himself. Thomas's response brings the Gospel back to its beginning as he recognizes Jesus not simply as a teacher, but as "My Lord and my God!" (20:28; cf. 20:17, 1:1).

CONCLUSIONS

John's story rounds out the canonical accounts of Jesus's life, death, and resurrection. John's version clearly resonates with the previous Synoptic traditions but adds its own twist. Although all the Gospels emphasize the importance of Jesus's identity, John focuses on this theme so completely that it overshadows everything in this Gospel. There is little mention of the Kingdom of God. Instead, John repeatedly stresses the need to recognize and believe that Jesus is God's Son and Christ in order to receive eternal life (20:30–31). This life is "eternal" because it comes by participating in a unity with God, the Father, and Jesus as God's Son. The participation is enabled by the Holy Spirit, the other Advocate breathed out on the disciples by the resurrected Jesus in 20:22 (cf. Gen 2:7). With this Spirit filling Jesus's disciples, John ends the Gospel as it began: with imagery from Genesis. In the prologue, the Word was the means of God's creating and sustaining life in the beginning; in the Gospel proper, Jesus as the incarnate Word gives life to those who will receive it from him; and after his resurrection, Jesus breathes life into his disciples. The believers who come after these first disciples are included in this new creation when they receive the word the disciples speak (17:20). It is no wonder John's Gospel appeals to the mystical and philosophically minded. Its image is of a spiritual community united in seeking to love by imitating their departed leader and following teachings he descended from heaven to reveal before returning to the Father's bosom (1:18).

When we come to John now, we inherit it after a long history of complicated interpretations. The central controversy remains Jesus's identity, but many conflicts over interpretations of Jesus have fueled not love, but division and even violence. We don't have to look far to see how John's characterization of the Jews has been used by Christians throughout history to justify anti-Semitic actions and teachings. Such readings of John's story, however, distort the Gospel's original meanings because it ignores its ancient context. This Gospel was written by and for believers who felt marginalized and were certainly outnumbered in the Roman Empire. The fact that early believers had close Jewish ties should also clarify our readings. When reading John today, Christians need to be careful because Christianity and Judaism are two different religions. Moreover, Christians are now the majority culture in the West. John commands that Christians love and serve others, not judge and condemn them.

Apocryphal Gospels and Acts

Stories beyond the New Testament

WITH THE END OF THE Gospel of John, it might seem that our exploration of early Christian gospels and acts should be complete. Yet even though these five books became part of the NT canon, they were not the only gospels and acts written by early Christians. Even after early Christian leaders were coming to agree upon the four canonical Gospels and book of Acts, other Christians continued sharing and writing stories about Jesus and his first apostles. These stories were popular throughout Christian traditions, both Eastern and Western, into the Middle Ages. These works were suppressed, however, in the wake of the Protestant Reformation, which emphasized the importance of canonized texts rather than extracanonical writings and traditions. Dubbed "apocryphal," meaning "secret" or "hidden," these writings were largely ignored by biblical scholars, who likewise focused on canonical texts. Eventually the noncanonical works were collected and often printed as "New Testament Apocrypha" or, more recently, "Christian Apocrypha" to distinguish them from canonized works.[1]

The Christian Apocrypha includes several gospels and acts that harmonize and expand on the traditions preserved in the canonized versions. Their popularity even past the time of a more

An Introduction to the Gospels and Acts. Alicia D. Myers, Oxford University Press. © Oxford University Press 2022. DOI: 10.1093/oso/9780190926809.003.0007

settled canon provides insight into how Christians interpreted their faith long after the NT writings were composed. This chapter will differ from the format of the previous ones because it deals with the question of canon formation and summarizes many of the apocryphal works instead of focusing on a single writing. I will begin with a brief overview of the process of NT canonization before digging into the apocryphal gospels and acts themselves. These writings, while not in the Christian canon, should be partners in our conversations about the canonical Gospels and Acts. Often compared to contemporary fan fiction, the apocryphal gospels and acts give insight into some of the earliest interpretations of their canonized counterparts. In these writings, Christians fill in narrative gaps and apply Jesus's and his apostles' teachings in their changing world.[2] More than just entertaining, the apocryphal gospels and acts remind us of the diversity of early Christianity and the flexibility of canon among ancient Christians.

CONTEXTUALIZING THE CONVERSATION

The Bible is made up of many different books, written, edited, and interpreted over many years by diverse people and communities. The NT is just a part of the Christian Bible, and the Gospels and Acts only a smaller segment of that collection. When we focus too much on the Christian Bible as a whole, we not only lose sight of the significance of the individual books it contains, but also the fact that these were neither the *only* books Christians wrote nor the *only* ones from which Christians could choose to create their canon.[3] In fact, after studying the Gospels in this book, we might well wonder why Christians decided they needed a canon in the first place. After all, Jesus taught of his soon return (*Parousia*) in the Gospels (e.g., Mark 8:38–9:1, 14:62). So why, then, did Christians need an agreed-upon collection of authoritative writings?

The most immediate answer to this question is the "delay of the *Parousia*" or, more simply, the fact that Jesus hadn't returned yet. For early Christians who expected Jesus's imminent return, the passage of time was challenging and even traumatic. During this time the first, second, and third generations of Christians died, sometimes in violent and sporadic moments of persecution and sometimes just due to accidents, old age, childbirth, or disease (cf. 1 Thess 4:13–18). As time continued to pass, believers wrestled with what to do in the interim, as well as with questions of focus and understanding: Should they just wait for Jesus's return, or should they put their energies elsewhere, such as into ethics or evangelism? Maybe Jesus wasn't going to return at all, at least not in any physical way, so perhaps Christians just needed the Spirit instead? Even working through the canonical Gospels and Acts we see a shift in the urgency surrounding Jesus's return. Mark emphasizes Jesus's pending return, while Luke-Acts and John turn instead to highlight the role of the Holy Spirit as Jesus's continued presence among believers who live in the world. For John and Luke, Jesus will return, but believers shouldn't waste their time waiting on a hillside for that to happen (Acts 1:11).

Just as the NT writings address Jesus's return differently, so too did additional groups of Christians. These varied perspectives eventually led to internal debates as the Christian movement sorted out leadership and shaped what would become "orthodoxy" (right belief) and "orthopraxy" (right practice). Some Christians were labeled "docetic" or "gnostic," and believed Jesus's divinity precluded his being human or "fleshly" in any way. Others, called Ebionites, did not agree with Jesus's miraculous conception or other divine attributes; instead, Jesus was an inspired human prophet. A second-century bishop, Marcion, rejected the importance of Israel's Scriptures for Christians, arguing that the God of these writings was not the same as the Father of Jesus whom Christians worshiped. Marcion thought Christians should only read the Letters of Paul and an abridged version of the Gospel of Luke. In their rejection of Marcion's canon as too restrictive, other

Christian leaders realized they needed to reflect more seriously on which writings should be authoritative. On the other side, the Montanists (also second century CE) desired to have an expansive canon, claiming they had received special revelation of Jesus's return in Pergamum from the Holy Spirit. The Montanists' claims caused others to wrestle with limiting the canon, asking questions about the Holy Spirit's role and source: how should claims of inspiration be vetted in this young and rapidly expanding movement?[4]

Complicating all these questions was the separation of Christianity from developing Judaism after the First and Second Jewish Wars against Rome (66–73 CE, 132–35 CE). As Christianity and Judaism parted ways, Christians struggled to define their relationship with their mother faith, which often resulted in anti-Jewish polemic that haunted the growing movement and seeded later anti-Semitism that lingers even today. As the Christian movement became increasingly Gentile, animosity toward Jews increased in the writings of teachers later dubbed "apostolic," but it also appears in the apocryphal writings we will explore below.[5] Including these noncanonical writings in our discussion of the NT Gospels and Acts provides a more honest and comprehensive view of developing Christianity. Even when the NT canon seems settled, disputes continue and traditions develop, as any glance at the variety of Christian denominations in the world today can attest. We do well to remember that such debates and diversity of Christian expression stretch back into the beginning rather than emerging in the Reformation and modern eras. Christianity has always been a diverse faith and practice.

Digging Deeper: Three Criteria of Canonization

The canonization of the NT was a *process*, not an event. Even though church councils agreed upon a canon, they did so much later, the first time being at Carthage in 397 CE. When contemporary scholars look back on the formation of the Christian canon, they often highlight three criteria that seemed to influence the selection of books. These criteria, however, are *not* articulated as requirements for the inclusion of writings; they are only formulated in hindsight by scholars. They are, nevertheless, a helpful way for us to understand the priorities of ancient Christian leaders as they sifted through and reflected on which writings should be authoritative for all believers.

The first, and perhaps most important, criterion that emerges is *apostolicity*. "Apostolicity" refers to the likelihood that an apostle, or someone very close to an apostle, wrote or authorized the work. Related to apostolicity is the age of writings. Those with origins reaching back to the time of Jesus and his first disciples were often regarded as more authoritative and more likely to have some connection to the apostles (e.g., Luke 1:1–4). Several of the apocryphal writings we will explore below were censured in part because of their lack of apostolicity, or false attribution to an apostle, and most of these works were written at points too late for real consideration of canon inclusion.

The importance of apostolicity makes the inclusion of anonymous and pseudonymous writings in the NT as it now exists an interesting reality. The anonymous canonical Gospels have early connections to apostles (such as John Mark being the disciple of Peter, or Luke the companion of Paul) or are traditionally credited to apostles who walked with Jesus (Matthew and John). That contemporary scholars doubt these connections does not mean ancient Christian leaders did. Moreover, while contemporary understandings of authorship assume direct composition, ancient authorship was more about authority: apostolicity does not necessarily mean an apostle *wrote* the work, but that one stands behind it as the authoritative source.[6] As twenty-first-century readers, we have thoughts on the strengths of these connections, but time and distance preclude us from coming to certain conclusions.

Universality, or *catholicity*, was another criterion. These terms refer to the widespread geographical use and long-term applicability of writings. Writings used in important Christian centers were more likely to be authoritative, such as Antioch of Syria, Ephesus in Asia Minor, Alexandria in Egypt, Rome, and their surrounding environs. The more widespread writings were used for teaching congregations, the greater likelihood that church leaders agreed upon their contents. Approval and use by especially influential bishops in the large Christian centers meant a higher chance for writings to be included in emerging canon lists. Irenaeus of Lyons (ca. 120–203 CE), for example, argues for the authority of the four canonical Gospels and Acts against what he saw as heretical teachings, whether they were additional writings from Valentinus and other gnostics or the limitations set by Marcion (*Haer.* 3.11.8).

These same writings, however, also show us that Christians used works not ultimately included in the NT, such as *The Shepherd of Hermas* and the *Wisdom of Solomon*. Irenaeus and other Christian leaders used these works in their own writings when arguing with other Christians. Writing in the early fourth century, Eusebius of Caesarea reflects this diversity of sources by creating different categories of authority in his canon lists. He calls some works "recognized," meaning they are widely used to teach publicly in churches; others are "disputed," used by some teachers and not others; and some should be avoided altogether as "spurious" and "heretical" (*Hist. eccl.* 3.25.1–7). In these lists, the four Gospels and Acts are consistently listed as recognized works. Careful readers will notice, however, some writings that eventually became part of the NT are listed in the disputed and even spurious categories. Eusebius's lists are helpful in showing us that early Christians found early agreement on some writings, like the four Gospels and Acts, but they were not averse to incorporating writings they found edifying, even if they were not ultimately deemed "canonical." Some among them also avoided a few writings that later councils would recognize as canon. Indeed, even the works called "spurious" or "heretical" must also have had some traction for authors like Eusebius to repudiate their use.

The final criterion is *orthodoxy*. This category is especially slippery since there was no official orthodoxy at the beginning of the

Christian movement! Instead, believers, and especially those who became leaders, were establishing orthodoxy through debates, lived practice, and disputes, which NT texts themselves also indicate (Acts 11–15; Galatians 1–2; etc.). Recall that what we call "religions" were most often expressions of inherited practices rather than chosen beliefs in the ancient Mediterranean world. The importance of choosing to confess Christ and the development of "right doctrine" in emergent Christianity were something of a novelty and, as such, hotly contested.[7] Since being Christian did not depend on ancestry, gender, or social status, beliefs became more important as a litmus test determining who was "in" and "out" of God's Kingdom. Creeds did not come to dominate this discussion until the fourth century CE, but creed- and hymn-like statements in NT show early believers debating what would become key doctrinal statements (e.g., Phil 2:6–11; 1 Tim 6:11–16; 1 John 2:18–27).

As early as the late second century, certain Christian bishops affirmed a rule of faith (*regula fidei*) against teachings they considered heretical. As mentioned above, contested issues included Jesus's divinity and humanity, the authenticity of his death and resurrection, and the time or reality of his return. Aside from the content of writings, who used which writings was equally important. If writings were associated with teachers of so-called heretical groups, they were more likely to be rejected. The five apocryphal books of acts discussed below, for example, were associated with the Manichaeans, a heretical sect of Christians from the third century founded by Mani, who called himself the "apostle of light." Their association with this group, as well as their later dates of composition and lack of apostolicity, all but guaranteed their exclusion from the NT.

The Christian Apocrypha: Part of the Process

Irenaeus was the first to join the terms "apocryphal and spurious writings" with heretical teachers (*Haer.* 1.20.1). Picking up on Irenaeus's language, later Christian leaders labeled writings "apocryphal" to denote their noncanonical status. Among these authors is Athanasius of Alexandria, whose 39th Festal (Easter) Letter in 367 CE contains the first list of NT works that coheres with the modern-day canon, although in a slightly different order.[8] Athanasius differentiated canonical writings from apocryphal writings, though the works he deemed "apocryphal" are associated with OT authors rather than NT ones.[9] For many Christian leaders of this time period, the canon remained fluid, even if they agreed upon the importance of the four canonical Gospels and Acts. While writings affirmed as canonical were approved for public church teaching, other writings were considered edifying for personal study. The development and later existence of a NT canon did not prevent the composition of these writings, or their continued use and popularity. Some of these apocryphal works were so popular that they were later edited to cohere with orthodoxy and continued to be used in feast day celebrations.

Many of the apocryphal gospels and acts were composed after Christian leaders had settled on the four Gospels and the Acts of the Apostles as uniquely inspired. In fact, many of the apocryphal works show the influence of the canonical writings with harmonizations and clarifications of their narratives. That stories about Jesus, his earthly family, and his earliest followers continued to be written into the fifth century and beyond shows believers did not feel limited by the canonization of certain texts over and against others. Instead, the apocryphal works continued to build on the agreed-upon versions, filling in gaps, fleshing out otherwise minor characters, and recasting the Christian story in new geographical and cultural settings.[10]

In these ways, the apocryphal writings do not challenge the canonical writings so much as show their pervasive influence and adoration among early believers who interpreted and reinterpreted them with their fan fiction. As with contemporary fan fiction, debated and alternative narratives are cast (and recast), but the conflicts and editions rely on shared source texts and show the value placed on them by diverse communities. Rather than remaining silent, early Christians added to and reflected on their sacred stories about Jesus and his followers. These new stories connected believers to their Christian ancestors and maintained the relevance of beliefs and practices in a changing world.

TURNING TO THE TEXTS

The following summary will introduce you to some of the best-known apocryphal gospels and acts. This short overview is too brief to give each writing adequate attention, or even to name all the apocryphal gospels and acts, but it will give you a foundation from which to begin further study. We will start with the apocryphal gospels before turning to the apocryphal acts.

Apocryphal Gospels

Scholars have discovered and cataloged a number of apocryphal gospels, found in piles of remnant papyrus scraps at ancient monasteries, and in celebrated archaeological discoveries.[11] While it might surprise readers today, there is a wide variety of noncanonical stories about Jesus's life. We loosely identify these writings as "gospels" even though they often do not replicate the literary form we find in the canonical Gospels. Rather than ancient biographies, the apocryphal gospels feature novelistic episodes from Jesus's life or collections of teachings. Most often scholars categorize these works by the stage of Jesus's life on which they focus: (1) Jesus's infancy and childhood, (2) his ministry and collected sayings, and (3) his passion, resurrection, and postresurrection teachings.[12]

The first grouping of apocryphal gospels is sometimes called the "infancy gospels," since they record Jesus's conception and birth, as well as his childhood.[13] Perhaps the best-known of these focuses not so much on Jesus as on his mother, Mary, narrating her own life in order to explain why she was chosen to be Jesus's mother. Written as early as the second century, the *Protoevangelium of James* is a pre-gospel (*proto*) that retells Mary's miraculous birth, her childhood set apart as a maiden in the Jerusalem temple, her unusual betrothal to a much older widower named Joseph, and the scandal that resulted from her unexpected pregnancy. Throughout *Prot. Jas.*, Mary's purity and righteousness are paramount; her virginity is intact even *after* she births Jesus in a painless glow of light (19.2)! While the Gospel of Luke leaves Mary's character ambiguous, *Prot. Jas.* explains why she was chosen by God as a worthy mother to his Son. The popularity of *Prot. Jas.* is evidenced not only in the large number of manuscripts that preserve it, but also in later Christian doctrines that proclaim Mary's perpetual virginity and in art that portrays her giving birth not in a manger, but in a cave (18.1, Figure 7.1).

Another well-known, and perhaps infamous, work records Jesus's life as a child, especially how he engaged with other children and adults while knowing himself to be the divine Son of God. Composed in the late second or third century, the *Infancy Gospel*

FIGURE 7.1 *The Nativity with the Prophets Isaiah and Ezekiel*, by Duccio di Buoninsegna (1255–1319). National Gallery of Art. Wikimedia Commons. Public Domain.

of Thomas emphasizes Jesus's divinity and, therefore, his superiority to all he meets. The clash between humans and the divine Jesus often leads to disastrous consequences. Jesus regularly defies his father by using miracles to dodge sabbath observance and insulting his tutors. He even murders other children who interfere with him! Repeatedly characters say of Jesus, "This child is not earth born" and that "every word he speaks, whether good or evil, was a deed and became a miracle" (5.2, 7.2).[14] Child Jesus is not, however, always cruel; he also resurrects and heals those injured in accidents, and he relents when others acknowledge his superiority. Influenced by the Gospel of Luke, *Inf. Gos. Thom.* portrays a special relationship between Jesus and his mother, ending with the story of their traveling to Jerusalem for Passover when Jesus was twelve. As in Luke, *Inf. Gos. Thom.* ends with a description that Mary "stored up all that had taken place" and confirms Jesus's continued growth in "wisdom and stature and grace" (19.5; cf. Luke 2:51–52).

The second group of apocryphal gospels records Jesus's teachings, but many of these have not survived in full form. The best-known example is the *Gospel of Thomas*. Different from *Inf. Gos. Thom.* described above, *Gos. Thom.* is a collection of sayings ascribed to Jesus. Although its completed form is often dated to the mid-second century, many of the sayings show remarkable similarity to the Synoptic Gospels.[15] For this reason, scholars suggest some sayings in *Gos. Thom.* may come from Jesus himself. The sayings are esoteric in nature, meant for the already initiated, and describe a type of secret knowledge given by Jesus. The *Gos. Thom.* is, therefore, described as "gnostic" because it portrays Jesus as a divine teacher providing knowledge (*gnosis*) needed for spiritual salvation. This particular gnostic tradition requires ascetic living, but not all gnostic Christians would agree with this focus.[16] Among the most perplexing sayings in *Gos. Thom.* are those about infants and women. Mary Magdalene plays a prominent role and is assured of salvation by being "made male" by Jesus's teaching in logion 114. Rather than a change of biological gender, Jesus's saying could indicate a type of masculinization for Mary according to ancient Roman-era norms that aligned rationality, self-control, and perfection with masculinity and ideal "maleness."[17]

The third, and final, group of apocryphal Gospels are those that retell Jesus's passion, resurrection, and teachings in postresurrection appearances. This group similarly fills in gaps missing from the canonical accounts, providing either greater detail about Jesus's crucifixion or focusing on minor characters, such as Joseph of Arimathea and Nicodemus, who appear in the passion accounts. There is also a remarkable thread in these writings that seeks to vindicate Pilate and, as such, exposes the growing anti-Jewishness of early Christianity. The most prominent of these traditions is the Pilate Cycle (ca. fifth–sixth century), which presents Pilate as a sympathetic character and convert to Christ.[18] Much earlier, however, is the *Gospel of Peter* (second century), which only survives in fragments. This story retells Jesus's crucifixion, blending the four canonical accounts but augmenting them with greater detail and offering a sympathetic Pilate. Rather than Pilate, King Herod (Antipas) orders Jesus's crucifixion, while Pilate famously washes his hands (*G. Pet.* 1.1; Matt 27:24). When Pilate receives a report from his soldiers about Jesus's resurrection, he states, "I am clean from the blood of the Son of God; it was you who desired it" (*G. Pet.* 11.46; cf. Matt 27:62–28:15).

The *Gospel of Peter* describes additional events narrated in Matthew 27, adding significantly more detail to the moment of Jesus's resurrection. Instead of just an earthquake and sudden moving of the stone, the soldiers in *Gos. Pet.* also witness a bright light coming from the tomb as three men, as well as the cross on which Jesus was crucified, walk out of it (9.34–11.44). The three men appear as giants, with Jesus the tallest of the three. Jesus's head reaches beyond the heavens, but he is supported by the two other men, usually interpreted as the angels who figure in other Gospel accounts (Luke 24:4; John 20:12; cf. Mark 16:5; Matt 28:2). In this well-known scene, either the cross itself or Jesus ("the crucified one") affirms Jesus's preaching to "those who sleep," that is, those who are dead.[19] This clear reference to 1 Pet 3:19 reflects the Petrine attribution of this apocryphal gospel as well as early interest in how Jesus spent his time among the dead.

Christ's Descent into Hell, a part of The Pilate Cycle, develops this tradition further by providing a detailed and entertaining account of Jesus's arrival in Hades ("Death"), which is both a place and a character in the story. In this account, Hades and the Devil debate back and forth about Jesus's coming even before he arrives. Hades does not want to take Jesus into himself because he can tell something is different about him. The Devil, however, thinks Jesus is just an ordinary human, and therefore, guilty of sin. According to the Devil, Hades can safely consume Jesus, adding to his grotesque collection of dead. Yet, when Jesus arrives, Hades's worst fears are realized and the Devil is shown to be a fool. As the sinless Son of God, the Devil has no authority over Jesus. Moreover, Jesus has the power to storm the gates of Hades and force his way in. Once he opens Hades's gates—or mouth—Jesus frees all the trapped souls, emptying the gluttonous Hades and leaving him to bicker with the outwitted Devil, while Jesus takes the freed souls to Paradise!

Jesus's postresurrection teachings were also a popular topic for apocryphal gospels, including other so-called gnostic gospels.[20] Like *Gos. Thom.*, these writings emphasize the superior knowledge Jesus provides for the inner peace and salvation of his followers. Included among these gospels is the fragmented *Gospel of Mary*, dating to the second century and the only gospel attributed to a woman. This Mary is Mary Magdalene, the only Mary who appears in every empty tomb scene in the canonical Gospels (Mark 16: 1–8; Matt 28:1–10; Luke 24:1–12; John 20:11–18). Although Mary's actual authorship of this gospel is unlikely, the connection shows her important role in early Christianity.[21] In *Gos. Mary*, Mary shares special revelations the risen Jesus gave her alongside his command for her to proclaim his resurrection. Although initially skeptical, the disciples eventually accept Mary's words once Levi (Matthew) acknowledges, "The Savior made her worthy" (9.8).

Altogether, these apocryphal gospels show continued interest in understanding Jesus, especially the parts of his life and teaching left out of the canonical Gospels. Early Christians, just like contemporary ones, wondered about Jesus's earthly family, his childhood, and earliest disciples. They wondered if there were more teachings from Jesus they could learn and wanted more details about his crucifixion and resurrection. All these questions, and the writings that emerged from them, are relatable even though we might prefer different answers than what ancient Christians gave. The apocryphal gospels show early believers wrestling with the authoritative traditions even as they added to them in the centuries after Jesus's departure.

Apocryphal Acts

The apocryphal acts likewise develop traditions from the canonical Gospels and the book of Acts. Rather than focusing on Jesus's life, however, these works describe fantastic journeys by several of the best-known apostles traveling to the limits of the known world, spreading the gospel message and working miracles. The apocryphal acts are best understood as legendary novels and even regularly use tropes common to Greco-Roman romance stories. The five outlined here are among the earliest surviving accounts and are often associated with the same author: Leucius, or Leucius Charinus, traditionally identified as a companion of John of Zebedee. There is no way to be certain of Leucius's authorship, or the reality of his association with John, but similar themes and events throughout these writings indicate some sort of relationship. Although debated, the usual order of composition suggested by scholars is (1) the *Acts of Paul*, which came to include the *Acts of Thecla* as well (abbr. *APT*, ca. 160); (2) *Acts of Peter* (ca. 150–200 CE); (3) *Acts of John* (ca. 180–200 CE); (4) *Acts of Thomas* (ca. 200–225 CE); and (5) *Acts of Andrew* (ca. 260 CE), which has a number of later additions and revised versions.[22] These writings were collected as a group and used by Manichaean Christians, a heretical gnostic group, thus encouraging proto-orthodox Christians to reject their authority. Their popularity, however, is attested by the survival of these stories in hagiographies, authorized revisions, and summarized versions in diverse languages.

In each of these novelistic stories, the apostles travel in accordance with the Lord's command (Matt 28:19–20; Acts 1:8), although Thomas needs extra encouragement to do so. Like the wayward Jonah, Thomas seeks to avoid his trip, but Jesus appears and sells him as a slave to force him to travel with his new master to India (*Acts Thom.* 1–2)! The other apostles are generally more willing to travel, though they might need some encouragement to remain with converts who had previously tortured them (*Acts Andr. Mth.* 33). The *Acts of Paul* describes his travels throughout Greece and Asia Minor, as well as Syria, before he eventually arrives in Rome, where he is martyred. Peter, too, spends time in Rome after being summoned there to care for Paul's converts after his departure to Spain. The *Acts of Peter* expands on Peter's rivalry with Simon Magus from Acts 8, and includes miracles of talking dogs, infants, resurrections, and even a flying Simon before Peter ultimately defeats him. Peter's story also ends with his famous martyrdom when he is crucified upside down (*Acts Pet.* 30–41). John spends his time in Asia Minor, especially Ephesus, repeatedly resurrecting people in order to gather converts and preaching sexual abstinence. Andrew travels to Greece, though traditions also describe his travels further north and eastward into Scythia (modern-day Russia). Andrew is often overlooked in the West, where Peter's traditional role as the first bishop of Rome paved the way for the Roman Catholic papacy. Andrew, however, is the more significant apostle in the East. As Peter's brother, and potentially the first of Jesus's disciples (John 1:40–42), Andrew was credited with founding the Byzantium church and became the apostolic ancestor of the ecumenical Orthodox patriarch of Constantinople, the Orthodox counterpart to the pope.

The traveling apostles experience visitations from Jesus and perform miracles, frequently asking God to give signs through them to convince people to convert. Among the repeated storylines in these acts is the conflict a traveling apostle creates within the household of an influential man. When apostles arrive in town, their miracles and preaching attract attention from regular people, but also from well-placed women, the concubines and wives of powerful men. The apocryphal acts share a common disdain for sex, even sex within marriage, referring to it as "filthy intercourse" or "lust" (*Acts Thom.* 12, 13; *Acts John* 69; *Acts Andr.* 14–16). The apostles preach against all sex, calling children distractions from a spiritual life and even ascribing to Jesus a discourse on the problems children bring (*Acts Thom.* 12)! When the women convert to Christianity, therefore, they stop having sex with their husbands or break off engagements with a fiancé, which causes significant conflict (*APT* 5, 12–15, 19). For some husbands, their wives' new faith leads to their conversions, while for others, it becomes the reason they execute the apostles (*Acts Pet.* 34; *Acts Andr.* 27; *Acts Thom.* 159–70).

The focus on women in these writings reflects the general polemic against early Christians in the Roman Empire: that they were homewreckers.[23] Yet this focus might also reflect a high inclusion of women in the early Christian movement, as well as some of the real-world consequences of their conversions. Indeed, several canonical writings indicate trouble caused when wives converted without their husbands (1 Pet 3:1–2) as well as a desire for Christian wives to cohere with Roman moral expectations (1 Tim 2:8–15). In the apocryphal acts, the women's abstinence does not remove sexual language or imagery from the story. Instead, as in other Greco-Roman novels, there is a preoccupation with sex, but the intercourse presented shifts. Instead of seeking husbands, the women's affections are given to alternative partners: the apostles over whom they dote and whom they allow into their chambers, and to Jesus, who is characterized as their spiritual husband, far superior to any human man.

The attention to women in these writings, however, is far from singularly positive. Women are regularly portrayed as temptations to men, and several pray for their own deaths, or are divinely maimed, to prevent their leading men to stray with sexual desire.[24] Peter's ten-year-old daughter, for example, was such a great temptation to a grown Roman man that her father rejoiced when she returned miraculously paralyzed, and thus not raped, after being kidnapped by her pursuer. Although Peter demonstrates his ability to heal her, he returns her to a paralyzed state because he believes it to be the Lord's will.[25] Furthermore, the supposed concern for the purity of noble and freeborn girls and women in these writings is not extended to slaves. Instead, slaves are regularly cast as negative foils for the righteous women they serve, even being disguised and used as sexual stand-ins to facilitate a wife's abstinence (*Acts Andr.* 17–22). The writings also cast blackness as ugly and evil, aligning whiteness with light and purity (*Acts Pet.* 22). Although not the same as what eventually became racism in the United States, the sorts of depictions in the apocryphal acts show the depth of racist tendencies in Christian traditions that should be acknowledged. As with their preoccupation with sex, these classist and ethnic stereotypes likewise replicate the tropes of Greco-Roman novels.

One woman's story recorded in these acts is that of Thecla, a noblewoman from Iconium who refuses to marry her powerful fiancé after being converted by Paul's teaching on virginity. Thecla deserves special mention because of the popularity of her story, which may have also circulated separately from the *Acts of Paul.* Although Paul's disciple, Thecla quickly finds herself on her own, needing to rely on God as her protector during not one, but two, arena scenes: one in Iconium, where her own mother called for her to be burned alive (*APT* 20); and one in Antioch, where her attempted rapist seeks to have her slaughtered by wild beasts (26–27). Thecla survives each of these encounters, even using the water in the second arena to baptize herself after Paul refused to do so back in Iconium (34). When Thecla returns to Paul with her own disciples, having cut her hair and dressed as a man, he acknowledges her gifts and authorizes her to continue teaching (40–41). She eventually settles in Seleucia, where she continued teaching and gathering disciples until her death (43). Thecla's popularity led to shrines at Seleucia and her portrait being included alongside that of Paul's in ancient frescos.[26] The third-century Latin church father, Tertullian, explicitly condemns Thecla because of her gender and self-baptism (*On Baptism*, 17), but the fact that he had to do so is further support of her widespread and lasting influence.

Although not known by many Western Christians, especially Protestants, these stories were important to the burgeoning Christian movement as believers developed their faith traditions beyond the canonical Acts. These stories show how early Christians dealt with the gaps left by what came to be the canonical writings—filling in missing stories about Jesus's chosen Twelve Apostles, as well as their very first converts. Several of these traditions remain mainstays in larger Christian circles, such as the martyrdom of Peter and Paul in Rome during the reign of Nero, the association of Thomas with India, and the importance of Andrew as Jesus's apostle and Peter's brother. The focus on women and sex also shows us the struggles Christians had in deciding how to live as disciples: what should their ethics look like in a Roman world? And how can a faith with many women converts be trustworthy? While orthodox Christianity eventually came to reject the authority of these stories, they give us glimpses of the diversity of ancient Christianity. Providing images of popular piety, these writings show how early Christians received and reshaped traditions in order to apply them in contexts and cultures far beyond the NT itself.

CONCLUSIONS

Although brief, this overview should demonstrate the importance of the apocryphal gospels and acts. While they are extracanonical, they are also part of the larger phenomenon of early Christian writings. Christian apocryphal writings expand on canonical works, giving more information on Jesus's childhood, family, teachings, and apostles. These writings contain a variety of fascinating stories that reveal how early Christians wrestled with questions about Jesus's identity, how to live a holy life in the Roman Empire, and how their faith spread to other lands. In all these stories, God guides believers through teachers and miraculous rescues. Rather than focusing on Jesus's imminent return, believers in the apocryphal gospels and acts are committed to living holy lives, separated from Roman extravagance, in hopes of attaining a blessed afterlife.

The comparison of the apocryphal gospels and acts to contemporary fan fiction might be simplistic, but it is also helpful. Fan fiction may stray from a recognized canon, but it is also dependent on a canon and a commitment to a basic story at its core. In the same way, the apocryphal gospels and acts are committed to the stories preserved in their canonized counterparts, even though they add to and answer questions left open in those same writings. Although later Christians came to disagree with the answers these writings offer, the apocryphal gospels and acts tackle questions readers of the NT still have today. By writing stories that seek to flesh out traditions and make them understandable in later contexts, early Christians were wrestling with their own faith commitments, especially as they continued to await and debate Jesus's return.

The Christian Apocrypha reminds us that the closing of the canon does not equate to a closing of interpretations. In fact, "closing" a canon simply refines the number of texts and traditions to be expanded upon by later authors and storytellers! Even today, Christians do not operate with *only* the canonized writings. Instead, different Christian traditions, churches, and individual believers approach their Bibles with a preference for some writings and an aversion for others—Matthew over Mark, or John rather than Luke. This, sometimes unintentional, practice creates a "canon within a canon" where one set of writings, or even an entire testament, is emphasized while others remain unread or underexplored. Beyond Christian canons, authors continue to write introductions, produce church orders, and craft devotional materials and commentaries interpreting biblical texts to make them accessible to contemporary audiences. Rather than a new activity, contemporary extracanonical writings build on a long-standing tradition of Christians writing, and rewriting, stories in order to remember their heroes and to practice their faith in new cultural contexts.[27]

8

Conclusion

Reading the Gospels and Acts Today

IN THIS SHORT BOOK, WE have covered a lot of ground together. We focused on the canonical Gospels and the book of
Acts, seeing how these works portray Jesus in similar and different ways and reflecting their first-century contexts. Although
retelling the life of the same Jesus of Nazareth, each of the canonical Gospels has different emphases in its depiction. The Gospel
of Mark, the earliest of the four canonized accounts, gives us
the shortest version of events. Mark portrays Jesus as an apocalyptic prophet ushering in God's Kingdom with his ministry
and crucifixion, to the astonishment of those around him. The
Gospel of Matthew expands on Mark, giving more attention to
Jesus's origins and the content of his teaching while rooting him
more firmly in his Jewish context. Although Jesus's death is still
surprising, Matthew adds accounts to verify Jesus's resurrection
and to commission the Gospel audience to continue their lives
of discipleship. Luke, likewise, expands on Mark, and perhaps
Matthew as well. As in Matthew, Luke gives more attention to
Jesus's origins and teachings, but the overall portrayal is centered
on the marginalized whom Jesus heals and welcomes. The book of
Acts extends this welcome yet further as the disciples learn God
welcomes Gentiles into the Kingdom, showing divine hospitality
that the disciples are also meant to imitate. The Gospel of John
builds on these themes, but again offers its own take on the story.
Probably influenced by the Synoptic traditions that came before,

An Introduction to the Gospels and Acts. Alicia D. Myers, Oxford University Press. © Oxford University
Press 2022. DOI: 10.1093/oso/9780190926809.003.0008

John's Gospel presents a more divine and philosophical Jesus who is unrecognizable without human humility and God's help. With its emphasis on the Holy Spirit and the Gospel's witness, John encourages its audience to be faithful even though the world in which they find themselves is still unable to recognize the Savior who visited them.

We also added a look at some apocryphal gospels and acts to show the breadth of early Christian writings and experiences. Although surprising for many contemporary readers, ancient Christians did not hesitate to expand on the writings that eventually made it into the NT canon. These later writings often harmonize the canonical Gospels and Acts, and then build on the traditions described in them by answering open-ended questions or completing a story the writings began. Instead of challenging the canon, these works show the importance of the canonical works and the different ways ancient Christians wrestled with them. As a type of ancient fan fiction, these works illustrate how early Christians struggled to live faithful lives in a Roman world even as they waited for, and debated, Jesus's return.

While fascinating, all these stories are ancient ones, the most recent ones having been written over fifteen hundred years ago. What can these old stories, and the interpretations of them, teach us that is relevant today? And what can they actually tell us that is historically reliable about Jesus of Nazareth and the religious movement he inspired? Hopefully, the information contextualizing the compositions and the short summaries at the end of each chapter have prompted possible answers to these questions but, for some of you, this information may have just muddied the waters further. We have reflected on the Gospels and Acts separately, but now it's time to bring them back together to think through their implications for today. This final chapter will do just that, working in three main sections: "Questions about the Historical Jesus," "Questions of Continued Relevance," and "Lessons for Reading the New Testament."

QUESTIONS ABOUT
THE HISTORICAL JESUS

One of the most pressing questions my students have about the canonical Gospels is their historicity, especially in their portrayals of Jesus. Reading carefully, this might be the first time you noticed how different each of the canonical Gospels is from the others, not to mention the complications brought about by the book of Acts. If these writings don't match up, how can we trust anything in them?

Like many questions we've had throughout this study, this one has also garnered the attention of plenty of biblical scholars. Beginning in eighteenth-century Germany, H. S. Reimarus started the original quest for the historical Jesus.[1] This doesn't mean Reimarus was the first to ask historical questions about Jesus and his presentation in the Gospels, but rather that he was one of the first to use Enlightenment methods and assumptions to aid that quest. For Reimarus, and many who followed in his footsteps, the historical Jesus of Nazareth was distinct from the Christ of faith created by church traditions of miracles, a virgin conception, and the resurrection. Influenced by Reimarus, his successors also used a modernist lens to discount as unhistorical anything that contradicted natural laws. For these first questers, the historical Jesus was a charismatic and apocalyptic Jewish man, whose visions of God's in-breaking Kingdom ended with his tragic death upon a cross.

Not surprisingly, many scholars and Christians were left unsatisfied by this first quest. Later questers sought to redeem the historical Jesus, often giving versions of his life that were less apocalyptic, less Jewish, and more in keeping with nineteenth- and twentieth-century morals in Western bourgeois societies. The fact that such work often resulted in a Jesus removed from his Jewish context had dire results. Combined with the long-term anti-Jewish and anti-Semitic threads of Christianity, a Jesus who combated Jews rather than existed as a Jewish man himself was used to justify further policies and violence against Jews into the twentieth century, even contributing to Nazism. The desire to rescue a failed historical Jesus, while seemingly admirable, was ultimately used to separate him from his own people.

In response, Ernst Käsemann initiated the creation of various criteria to find the historical Jesus, hoping a more scientific method would bring about more conclusive results.[2] Käsemann's first criterion was "dissimilarity," which suggests that stories of Jesus's words or actions that are both dissimilar to first-century Judaism and early Christianity are more likely to be historical. Later scholars added three more criteria: (1) embarrassment, which argues Jesus traditions that would have embarrassed early Christians are more likely to be historical; (2) multiple attestation, which argues the more independent sources in which a tradition appears, the more likely its historicity; and (3) coherence, meaning something that is consistent with the other criteria is more likely to be historical. Yet, even using agreed-upon criteria, scholars continued to produce lives of Jesus that more or less reflected their own values. These scholars still fell victim to Albert Schweitzer's incisive critique from 1906: scholars often create a historical Jesus who reflects their own image.[3]

So what is the way forward in all of this? Recognizing the troubling history of historical Jesus research, more recent scholars have sought to relocate Jesus in his Jewish context, even if that means a Jesus who is less palatable for contemporary readers. Dale Allison offers what I find to be the most helpful option for reconstructing glimpses of the historical Jesus. First, he notes the fallacy of a dichotomy between history and theology.[4] Instead, he emphasizes, history and theology are always intertwined. He explains, "The New Testament offers us neither the historical Jesus unsullied by Christian interests and beliefs and distortions nor Christian distortions and beliefs unsullied by the historical Jesus. For there was always a dialectic."[5]

What Allison means is that Jesus was a historical person, but also one that thought theologically and acted on those beliefs. His life was recorded by people who believed theological things about him, even if they also lived a historical existence with him. There is simply no teasing out theology from history, or history from theology; nor should there be. Such a dichotomy is itself unfaithful to the life that Jesus lived.

Second, Allison notes that we will never have enough information to fill in all the details about Jesus's life that we would like, but that shouldn't stop us from working with the materials we do have. We simply need to work responsibly and with humility. For Allison, this means focusing on generalizations in Jesus traditions, especially the canonized accounts, rather than on specifics that we cannot prove. Allison provides a summary of Jesus's teachings and works from the four canonical Gospels, though, admittedly with a heavy focus on the Synoptics. From these lists, he argues we can confidently assert the following about Jesus: (1) he valued caring for others and self-sacrifice; (2) his outlook and teachings were eschatological, influenced by the apocalyptic Judaism of his day; and (3) Jesus had a reputation, and understood himself, as a miracle worker.[6] For Allison, therefore, past studies on the historical Jesus offer Christologies that are both too high and too low.[7] Those who affirm a Jesus who matches later Trinitarian orthodoxy are overconfident in asserting what we cannot know from the canonical witnesses. Those who present an ethical Jesus devoid of eschatology and miracles, however, are also overconfident, but this time in their own rationalist assumptions against apocalypticism and miracles. Instead, Jesus of Nazareth, who was later confessed as the Christ by his disciples, was an apocalyptic teacher and healer, who thought of himself and his ministry as crucial to the arrival of God's Kingdom in the world. Whether or not he was correct in that perception, however, is a question only one's faith perspective can answer.

What do Allison's conclusion mean, though, for the canonical Gospels and how we read them today? This question brings us back to my assertion at the beginning of this book: we need to read these ancient writings for what they are. Allison does not force the Gospels (or Acts) to be "historical accounts" in the contemporary sense. Instead, he approaches these writings as ancient biographies and historiographies, which means they adhere to different expectations than we have today. The Gospels and Acts contain historically accurate information, but this information has also been shaped to convey deeper truths from the author and his or her contexts. There is no separating history from theology, especially for a faith that eventually came to confess Jesus as God incarnate, coming into the world in order to save it. As I encouraged we do at the outset of our journey, therefore, we need to continue reading these works in light of their ancient circumstances and genres. We need to continue digging for more context, even though we will never recover all of it. What we do uncover, however, will help us interpret more responsibly and humbly. Given the powerful impacts past interpretations of these works have had, responsibility and humility are needed.

QUESTIONS OF CONTINUED RELEVANCE

Beyond questions of how the historical Jesus is reflected in the NT and extracanonical works, it's also fair to wonder exactly how these writings are still relevant today. Do these writings have anything to say in our current world? And how can we interpret them responsibly given their complicated history of interpretation and use in Western culture? For some of you, wondering about these questions might be a new (and perhaps even frightening) predicament. For others of you, you have long considered these questions, even if just in the back of your mind; and others—well, you answered them long ago. I want to approach them afresh here, building on the work we've done together in this book to read these writings in light of their ancient contexts. Retracking some of the ground covered in each chapter, we can make connections to contemporary situations that do not precisely mirror those of the ancient world, but that are similar to them. Moreover, a number of these contemporary issues are affected by the ways these very NT writings have been interpreted throughout history through today. The power of interpreting the NT Gospels and Acts means we must interpret with humility and responsibility, situating these writings in their world first before we translate meanings into ours.

In all the Gospels, but especially in the overview of Mark, we saw how religious practices and beliefs were connected to politics in the ancient Mediterranean world. Although Western societies often pride themselves on separating religion from state governments, this is a completely alien thought to the first century. The question "Was Jesus political?" simply doesn't make sense in the Gospels because there was no separation of politics and theology in the first century: theology was political, and politics were theological! This is a context where emperors claim to be appointed by gods and even exist as sons of a god. Likewise, Jesus claims to inaugurate the *Kingdom of God*; an alternative reign to the rule of Rome, which claims to govern the entire cosmos at the behest of its gods. Knowing the interrelationship, and indeed, interdependence of theology and politics in the first century helps us to appreciate and understand the Gospels and Acts better. We can see why Jesus was a threat to the Jerusalem leadership, both Jewish and Roman, and why the Roman government would have convicted him of sedition. It also shows us the legitimacy of the Jewish leadership's fear of Jesus and his followers: they knew what Rome did to rebellious peoples. The Gospels and Acts alone cannot give us that whole story, but digging into the historical and political realities of the Second Temple period gives us more of it.

The implications of this research in contemporary contexts are at least twofold: first, it unmasks the falsehoods of "pure" theology and "pure" politics. There are no such things. Instead, theologies impact politics and politics impact theologies. Anyone living in twenty-first-century Western contexts should certainly see this when political leaders leverage theological stances for election, and religious organizations leverage relationships to push for policies. The Gospels and Acts encourage this sort of overlap because they suggest one's actions should reflect a belief in Jesus as Messiah, especially his self-sacrifice. The NT writings, however, were composed at a time when Jews and Jewish Christians were in the extreme minority rather than the majority. In contrast, contemporary Western cultures often reflect a majority, culturally Christian stance. What would these authors and communities have to say to us now about politics, theology, and the care for others?

Second, knowing the political realities of the first century should combat the reflexive and often unconscious anti-Judaism of NT interpretation. This second implication blends into our discussion of ancient Judaism in the Gospel of Matthew. Rather than reading the NT Gospels and Acts as "Christian" works, we need to read them as part of the diverse Jewish writings from the Second Temple period and beyond. These works are part of intra-Jewish dialogues and debates about the Messiah and God's Kingdom. Recent work on social identity theory is helpful in showing us how we are often harsher toward members of our own in-groups (e.g., our family) than those on the outside. This helps to explain the polemic of Matthew, as well as all the Gospels and Acts, toward the Jews who do not accept Jesus as the Messiah. At the same time, however, it does not excuse this language and behavior, especially now that Christianity and Judaism have become two separate religions. Given the troubling history of anti-Judaism in the West fueled by Christian interpretations of these very Gospels and Acts, we need to take care when we interpret them now. We see the beginnings of anti-Jewish trajectories in the NT Gospels and Acts that are picked up and expanded upon in the Christian Apocrypha. Identifying those threads and contextualizing them are big steps to both acknowledging the past and moving into a different future.

In the chapters on Luke and the book of Acts, we explored ancient notions of humanness and practices of hospitality; while reading John, we focused on the philosophical dimensions of Jesus's incarnation. There is a lot we could apply and learn from these angles of interpretation. In Luke and Acts, we see how Jesus repeatedly challenges Roman assumptions of worth, upending them to show how God welcomes all people in the Kingdom, especially those considered the least valuable to Rome. In Acts, even the disciples are challenged to see that God's pouring out the Spirit on "all flesh" really means on "all flesh" as new believers are welcomed into the fold. Luke's emphasis on God's openness and love toward all people is a lesson we certainly can take forward in our own lives. John's Gospel reinforces this image of God with the incarnation. In John, God's Word leaves the divine realm to become flesh and reveal God's will in person. Rather than giving up on the world, God becomes manifest in it to reveal the magnitude of divine love. All three of these works caution us against dismissing "others" who are different from us as unworthy of our time or concern. They also rebuke the presumption of knowledge over humility. For Luke-Acts and John, people should remember their finitude and rely on a larger community attuned to the worth of all creation rather than just on those with whom they agree.

Finally, the Christian Apocrypha teaches us important lessons about the complexity of interpreting faith and traditions across cultures and time. Not all of the interpretations in these writings are admirable; indeed, many are offensive in their anti-Jewish, racist, and sexist views. Reading them, however, helps us to see better the questions early Christians had as time passed without Jesus's return and the movement became more and more Gentile-focused, eventually aligning itself with Roman rule. Within these writings, we see a growing concern for having right beliefs and living out ethical lives with the hopes of gaining eternal bliss after death. If we just focused on the canonical writings, we would miss how Christianity transformed from a primarily apocalyptic faith that looked for Jesus's rapid return, to a religion that focused on right belief and right practice to gain eternal life after death. While not all the interpretations in these writings are commendable, they provide vital insight into how the early church developed its doctrines, including its canon. The interpretations and choices made in these early centuries of the Christian movement shaped Western culture for centuries to come.

The thoughts given here just skim the surface of the ways in which the NT Gospels and Acts, as well as the Christian Apocrypha, remain relevant for us today. Even if these writings do not explicitly describe contemporary issues, they (or interpretations of them throughout history) have contributed to them in both positive and negative ways. Continuing to contextualize these writings and think about their history of interpretation enables us to understand our own contexts better, if not also our own beliefs.

LESSONS FOR READING THE NEW TESTAMENT

I would like to end this book with three final lessons for reading the NT more broadly. These lessons are applicable to reading anything deeply, however, so hopefully they will help you as you venture beyond the biblical horizon.

Lesson 1: Context Matters

This is by far the most important lesson of this book. A famous saying among biblical scholars is "A text without context is a pretext for a proof text." In other words, if I read a text without contextualizing it, then I can make it mean anything I want. The problems here are many, but one for sure is that it completely omits the past meanings of these works for their first authors and audiences. While we cannot recover what an author intended with absolute certainty, we can get an idea of how the Gospels and Acts were heard by various audiences in the Greco-Roman world. If we don't take the time to contextualize, we run the risk of misapplying texts and, worse, perpetuating harmful readings in our own day. For example, when we remember that Jesus was Jewish (and never Christian), that he ministered to Jews, and that his first followers were all Jewish, we can work to undo the conscious and unconscious anti-Judaism of many Christian interpretations.

In addition to ancient contexts, however, we also need to acknowledge and explore our own contexts, as well as those of others. We need to read in communities, rather than alone, hearing diverse perspectives and reactions to these profoundly influential texts. Reading and conversing with others face to face, through the pages of a book, or by listening to podcasts and online resources, we can see how much our context impacts our interpretations. Remaining in communities, especially diverse communities, helps to prevent us from myopic interpretations, deaf to the harmful implications of our assumptions as well as to the potentially liberative elements of these ancient works.

Lesson 2: Profound Difference and Profound Connection

Digging into the ancient contexts of the Gospels and Acts reveals profound differences between the Greco-Roman world and contemporary Western cultures. The assumptions about human worth, for example, come to mind immediately. The ancient Mediterranean world is deeply misogynistic and questions the value of disabled persons, while valuing wealth and self-control. Knowing these differences enables us to recognize the ways the NT Gospels and Acts push against ancient assumptions, as well as where they reinforce them. Jesus spends time with women, incorporates those with disabilities, teaches against accumulating outlandish wealth, and regularly undercuts people who seek control. At the same time, however, these writings often do not go as far in rectifying inequalities as we would like, and they still leave many people out of the discussion. Moreover, for all the differences, the problems faced in the Greco-Roman world resonate with many in our own; we still battle sexism, racism, ableism, and problems stemming from our fascination with wealth. Acknowledging the differences alongside the similarities helps us find meaning from these writings for issues we still face today.

Lesson 3: Acknowledge the Positives and the Negatives

Engaging with the Gospels and Acts in this book has uncovered both positive and negative implications and applications in Western culture. For some of you, the idea of negative implications from these writings is difficult, while for others, the positives might surprise you. As with the rest of human history and creations, the Gospels and Acts offer us a mixed bag of resources, which is why we must work to contextualize them and reflect on them. These writings have influenced the societies in which we live, both inspiring great actions of liberation and love *and* being used to justify oppression and violence.

Honest engagement with the Gospels and Acts, as well as the rest of the NT and other early Christian writings, should be a mix of charitable and critical reflection. We can be charitable by contextualizing these writings in their ancient milieu, understanding the culture and limitations of that world, while seeing within them a larger goal of bringing humanity closer to the divine. Critical reflection, however, means we must also name the limitations of these works, as well as the ways they have been interpreted irresponsibly and used to harm others. For Christians, this does not mean disregarding the NT as Scripture, but rather seeing it as one means of revelation about God rather than as a stand-in for God. As a faith centered on confessing Jesus as God become flesh, Christianity proclaims God's will to enter into the messiness of human history rather than remaining indifferent and detached.

As humans, we have no choice but to be a part of history, regardless of our faith confession. We are living out the consequences of choices made long before us and making choices that will impact generations long after we are gone. When we take the time to understand the writings and movements that shaped the world in which we live, we can make better choices and leave a better world for those who come after us. Reflecting on the Gospels and Acts in light of their ancient contexts, and with the community created by this book, has, I hope, changed how you read and interpret these writings. There is a bridge connecting you to the ancient world of the Gospels and Acts. This bridge is not a straight line, but rather has multiple twists, turns, ascents, cascading falls, and branches, bringing us to where we are in contemporary Western society. It's always been more complicated than we imagine, but we are still connected and can still learn from those who have gone before. I hope our journey through the Gospels and Acts has shown you a path forward on this complicated crossing, aiding you in creating a better world in the present and for ages to come.

NOTES

Chapter 1

1. The formation of the New Testament canon, as with the formation of the Christian canon overall, was a process rather than an event. In Chapter 7, I will discuss elements of this process, along with some of the Gospels and Acts that were not canonized.
2. *Acts of Thomas*, for example, describes Thomas's eastward journey spreading the gospel to India.
3. In addition to the complicated compositional history of the NT writings, they also have a complicated past in terms of preservation and transmission. There are thousands of existing manuscripts that regularly disagree, but which scholars have used to create the versions of the Greek NT we have today. The standard Greek NT text is the twenty-eighth edition of the Nestle-Aland (NA[28]).
4. For more background on these methods see Alicia D. Myers and Lindsey S. Jodrey, "Come and Read: Hermeneutics and Interpretive Perspectives in the Gospel of John," in *Come and Read: Interpretive Approaches to the Gospel of John*, ed. Alicia D. Myers and Lindsey S. Jodrey, IJL 1 (Baltimore, MD: Lexington Academic, 2020), 1–25.
5. Throughout this book, I will refer to Israel's Scriptures as the "Old Testament" (OT). It is crucial to remember that "Old Testament"

is a name given to these texts by later Christians, who came to understand their collection of writings as the "New Testament" (NT). In the NT writings themselves, these writings are the only extant "Scriptures" available. While "Old Testament" can be used in pejorative ways, that is not my intention here.

6. Gerhard Friedrich calls *euangelion* the "technical term for 'news of victory'" in battle ("εὐαγγέλιον," in *TDNT*, 2:722).

7. Friedrich, "εὐαγγέλιον," in *TDNT*, 2:723 (emphasis added).

8. All translations of the LXX are from *A New English Translation of the Septuagint*, ed. Albert Pietersma and Benjamin G. Wright (Oxford: Oxford University Press, 2007) unless otherwise noted. This translation is available online at http://ccat.sas.upenn.edu/nets/edition/.

9. In many English Bibles, the Greek word *christos* is translated as "Messiah," rather than "Christ" (see NRSV, NIV, NLT). While "Messiah" is a possible translation for the term, the inconsistent transitions from "Christ" to "Messiah" can mislead readers and obfuscate the confessions being made. In fact, there are only two verses where the Hebrew transliteration *messias* is used (John 1:41, 4:25)!

10. James D. G. Dunn, "The Gospel and the Gospels," *EQ* 85 (2013): 291–93.

11. Dunn argues that Paul is the one to introduce this term to the Christian tradition, but he does not seriously consider the possibility that Jesus could have used this term in his own lifetime ("The Gospel," 295–97). Jesus's use of "gospel" fits his proclamation of the Kingdom of God and influence by Isaiah, elements most historical Jesus scholars find credible (Dale C. Allison Jr., *Constructing Jesus: Memory, Imagination, and History* [Grand Rapids, MI: Baker Academic, 2010], 164–204).

12. Authorship in the ancient world is a sticky issue largely because contemporary readers assume a fixed state for written materials. We also assume the "author" is the person who physically wrote the work. In the ancient world, authors often worked with scribes who wrote for them. It is better to think if ancient authorship in terms of "authority" rather than as a single person responsible for written material.

13. Anthony Corbeill, "Education in the Roman Republic: Creating Traditions," in *Education in Greek and Roman Antiquity*, ed. Yun Lee Too (Leiden: Brill, 2001), 261–62. See more generally Judith Evans Grubbs and Tim Parkin, eds., *The Oxford Handbook on Childhood and Education in the Classical World* (Oxford: Oxford University Press, 2013). Michael L. Satlow highlights corresponding elements in Torah study in Jewish and later rabbinic contexts as well ("'Try to Be a Man': The Rabbinic Construction of Masculinity," *HTR* 89 [1996]: 22–35).

14. The Gospels also incorporate elements of other literary genres, but, on the whole, they most look like ancient biographies. Charles H. Talbert, *What Is a Gospel?* (Philadelphia: Fortress, 1977); Richard A. Burridge, *What Are the Gospels? A Comparison with Greco-Roman Biography*, 2nd ed. (Grand Rapids, MI: Eerdmans, 2004); Craig S. Keener, *Christobiography: Memory, History, and the Reliability of the Gospels* (Grand Rapids, MI: Eerdmans, 2019). The collection of anecdotes and stories about Jesus reflect general biographical and personal topoi from the ancient Roman world.

15. This is the classic distinction between biographies and historiographies. In practice, this distinction is often blurred, with biography existing as a subset of "historical narrative" (Theon, *Prog.* 78, 83, 104P; Ps.-Herm. *Prog.* 4; Libanius, *Prog.*; Lucian, *How to Write History*, 8–11, 43, 55–59; Arrian, *Anabasis of Alexander*). See also Philip Stadter, "Biography and History," in *A Companion to Greek and Roman Historiography*, ed. John Marincola, BCAW (Malden, MA: Blackwell, 2008), 528–31.

16. This list is from Aelius Theon's *Progymnasmata*, his collection of "preliminary exercises" for young rhetoricians. Theon's summary of topoi is very similar to those in other *progymnasmata*, rhetorical handbooks, and actual written works. Alicia D. Myers, *Characterizing Jesus: A Rhetorical Analysis of the Fourth Gospel's Use of Scripture in its Presentation of Jesus*, LNTS 458 (London: Bloomsbury T&T Clark, 2012), esp. 39–47.

17. On the importance of these three elements in ancient narratives see Myers, *Characterizing Jesus*, 27–35.

18. Allison, *Constructing Jesus*, 1–30.

19. Mark Goodacre, *The Case against Q: Studies in Markan Priority and the Synoptic Problem* (Harrisburg, PA: Trinity Press International, 2002), 19–45.

20. As recorded by Eusebius, *Hist. eccl.* 3.39.15.

21. Goodacre, *The Case against Q*; see also Michael Goulder, "Is Q a Juggernaut?," *JBL* 115 (1996): 667–81.

22. Matthew D. C. Larsen, *Gospels before the Book* (Oxford: Oxford University Press, 2018), 83–98.

23. Richard Bauckham, "For Whom Were the Gospels Written?," in *The Gospels for All Christians: Rethinking the Gospel Audiences*, ed. Richard Bauckham (Grand Rapids, MI: Eerdmans, 1998), 44–48; Chris Keith, *The Gospel as Manuscript: An Early History of the Jesus Tradition as Material Artifact* (Oxford: Oxford University Press, 2020), 82–85.

24. Keith, *The Gospel as Manuscript*, 101–59.

25. Robyn Faith Walsh, *The Origins of Early Christian Literature: Contextualizing the New Testament within Greco-Roman Literary Culture* (Cambridge: Cambridge University Press, 2021), 50–104; Richard Bauckham, "About People, by People, for People: Gospel Genre and Audiences," in Bauckham, *Gospels for All Christians*, 113–45.

26. Paul N. Anderson, *The Riddles of the Fourth Gospel: An Introduction to John* (Minneapolis: Fortress, 2011), 45–66; Tom Thatcher, *Why John Wrote a Gospel: Jesus—Memory—History* (Louisville: Westminster John Knox, 2006); Paul N. Anderson, Felix Just, and Tom Thatcher, eds., *John, Jesus, and History*, vol. 1: *Critical Appraisals of Critical Views*, SBLSymS 44 (Atlanta: SBL Press, 2007); Eve-Marie Becker, Helen K. Bond, and Catrin H. Williams, eds., *John's Transformation of Mark* (London: T&T Clark, 2021).

27. Paul N. Anderson, "The Community That Raymond Brown Left Behind: Reflections on the Johannine Dialectical Situation," in *Communities in Dispute: Current Scholarship on the Johannine Epistles*, ed. Alan R. Culpepper and Paul N. Anderson, ECL 13 (Atlanta: SBL Press, 2014), 72–77.

Chapter 2

1. For a booklike printing of Mark see David Rhoads, Joanna Dewey, and Donald Michie, *Mark as Story: An Introduction to the Narrative of a Gospel*, 3rd ed. (Minneapolis: Fortress, 2012).

2. Rhoads, *Mark as Story*; Elizabeth Struthers Malbon, *Hearing Mark: A Listener's Guide* (Harrisburg, PA: Trinity Press International, 2002); Thomas Boomershine's performance of Mark in English and Greek is available online: https://www.youtube.com/playlist?list=PL7DR0ecPG8I1WonZetQ6-Fj7gC4g4ED-L. Accessed 21 December 2020.

3. Eusebius, *Hist. eccl.* 2.15.1–2, 3.39.14–16; compare Justin Martyr, *Dial.* 106.3; Irenaeus, *Haer.* 3.1.1–2.

4. Joel Marcus, *Mark 1–8*, AB 27 (New York: Doubleday, 1999), 25–37.

5. Shaye J. D. Cohen, *From the Maccabees to the Mishnah*, 3rd ed. (Louisville: Westminster John Knox, 2014), 24–26.

6. Josephus was from a priestly family in Jerusalem, but eventually participated in the First Jewish War as a commander in Galilee. When he surrendered to the Romans, Josephus defected to their side and wrote against Jewish rebellion in his later historical works.

7. *Male* circumcision was especially difficult for Greeks and later Romans to understand since it was an unnecessary surgical procedure—thus risking infection without a clear cause—and effectively shortened or "mutilated" the penis. An erect penis was a ubiquitous symbol of power and protection in the ancient Mediterranean world; thus, cutting it was offensive for non-Jews.

8. John J. Collins, *The Apocalyptic Imagination: An Introduction to Jewish Apocalyptic Literature*, 2nd ed., BRS (Grand Rapids, MI: Eerdmans, 1998), 12–21.

9. On Mark's literary style see Mary Ann Tolbert, *Sowing the Gospel: Mark's World in Literary-Historical Perspective* (Minneapolis: Fortress, 1989); and the works of Elizabeth Struthers Malbon, most recently, *Mark's Jesus: Characterization as Narrative Christology* (Waco, TX: Baylor University Press, 2014).

10. The quotation in Mark 1:2 is a combination of Isa 40:3 and Mal 3:1. Joel Marcus, *The Way of the Lord: Christological Exegesis of the Old Testament in the Gospel of Mark* (Louisville: Westminster John Knox, 1992), 12–47.

11. Rikki E. Watts, *Isaiah's New Exodus and Mark*, BSL (Grand Rapids, MI: Baker Academic, 2001).

12. On spirit-possession in the ancient world see Pamela E. Kinlaw, *The Christ Is Jesus: Metamorphosis, Possession, and Johannine Christology*, SBLAB 18 (Atlanta: SBL Press, 2005), 41–67.

13. Compare Matthew 5–7; Marcus, *Mark 1–8*, 194–95.

14. Many interpreters note the irony of Jesus's mock coronation during his crucifixion in the canonical Gospels. Sharyn Dowd, *Reading Mark: A Literary and Theological Commentary on the Second Gospel*, RNT (Macon, GA: Smyth & Helwys, 2000), 156–63; Joel Marcus, "Crucifixion as Parodic Exaltation," *JBL* 125 (2006): 111–25.

15. *Mart. Isa.* 5.1–16; *Liv. Pro.* 1.1; Heb 11:37.

16. 2 Chr 33:6–12; *Pr. Man.*

17. Candida R. Moss, "Mark and Matthew," in *The Bible and Disability: A Commentary*, ed. Sarah J. Melcher, Mikeal C. Parsons, and Amos Yong (Waco, TX: Baylor University Press, 2017), 288–91.

18. See also Mark 12:10–11 (Ps 118:21–22). Marcus, *Way of the Lord*, 111–29.

19. Jesus makes no such claim in Mark. Instead, he claims to be the Son of Man from Dan 7:14. His confession before the high priest in Mark 14:62 contrasts with his commands for secrecy earlier in the narrative, signifying that *this* is the moment he has been predicting since Mark 8:30.

20. For more on the endings of Mark see Beverly Roberts Gaventa and Patrick D. Miller, eds., *The Endings of Mark and the Ends of God: Essays in Memory of Donald Harrisville Juel* (Louisville: Westminster John Knox, 2005).

21. Dennis Covington describes a history of these traditions in *Salvation on Sand Mountain: Snake Handling and Redemption in Southern Appalachia* (Philadelphia: Da Capo Press, 2009).

Chapter 3

1. All the canonical Gospels are Jewish, and they tell the story of Jesus, a Jewish man who had Jewish disciples and was responsible for a Jewish movement. Matthew's Gospel is often considered the most Jewish of the canonical accounts because of its extensive use of the OT, characterization of Jesus, and language about the "kingdom of heaven" rather than "kingdom of God."

2. See Chapter 2.

3. Krister Stendahl, *The School of St. Matthew and Its Use of the Old Testament*, 2nd ed. (Philadelphia: Fortress, 1968).

4. Richard Bauckham, "For Whom Were the Gospels Written?," in *The Gospels for All Christians: Rethinking the Gospel Audiences*, ed. Richard Bauckham (Grand Rapids, MI: Eerdmans, 1998), 44–48; Daniel W. Ulrich, "The Missional Audience of the Gospel of Matthew," *CBQ* (2007): 66.

5. Antioch remains the most suggested provenance for the Gospel, though Galilee is also regularly suggested. David C. Sim, "The Gospel of Matthew and Galilee: An Evaluation of an Emerging Hypothesis," *ZNW* 107 (2016): 141–69, provides an overview of these arguments but judges Antioch remains the more convincing choice.

6. Magnus Zetterholm, "The Jews of Antioch after the Fall of Jerusalem," *Bible Odyssey*, https://www.bibleodyssey.org/en/places/related-articles/jews-of-antioch-after-the-fall-of-jerusalem, accessed 21 December 2020.

7. Once Christians were recognized as belonging to a different religious group than Jews, they lost the protection afforded by the antiquity of Jewish practices, and the relationship between the Romans and the Hasmoneans discussed in Chapter 2. While there was no widespread persecution of Christians until Decius (ca. 250 CE), there were localized prosecutions as early as the late first and early second centuries CE.

8. Shaye J. D. Cohen, *From the Maccabees to the Mishnah*, 3rd ed. (Louisville: Westminster John Knox, 2014), 53–102.

9. I'm using the term "school of thought" rather than "sect" because of the negative overtones this word has in English. As Cohen

observes, the terms we translate as "sect" or "heresy" were "neutral terms for 'school' (a collection of people) or 'school of thought' (a collection of ideas)" (*Maccabees*, 125).

10. Josephus, *J. A.* 13.15.5; 18.1.3–4.

11. *p. Avot.* 1.1; compare Josephus, *J. A.* 13.10.6.

12. Josephus, *J. A.* 18.1.3–4.

13. There were other temples outside of Jerusalem, including at Mount Gerizim in Samaria, the Temple of Onias, also called Leontopolis (*J. A.* 13.62–68; *J. W.* 7.426–32), and at Elephantine, both in Egypt.

14. Josephus, *J. A.* 18.1.5; *J. W.* 2.8.2–13.

15. To read the Dead Sea Scrolls in English see Florentino García Martínez and Eibert J. C. Tigchelaar, eds., *The Dead Sea Scrolls: Study Edition*, 2 vols. (Leiden: Brill; Grand Rapids, MI: Eerdmans, 1997).

16. Josephus, *J. A.* 18.1.6.

17. The Edomites were forced to convert to Judaism or leave their lands during the reign of the Hasmonean king, John Hyrcanus (ca. 134–104 BCE). For this reason, many did not consider Herod the Great authentically Jewish, although he was raised Jewish.

18. Missing from this list are (1) Herod II, who was the first husband to Herodias. He is confused with Herod Philip (Philip the Tetrarch) in Mark 6:17–18 and Matt 14:3–4, which Luke 3:19 seems to correct. Herod II was removed from his father's line of succession after his mother's participation in a failed coup attempt against his father. (2) Herod of Chalcis (Syria, r. ca. 42–48 CE), who is not mentioned in the NT but who was married to Bernice, the sister of Agrippa II (Acts 25:23–26:32).

19. While scholars debate the precise date of the parting of the ways between Christianity and Judaism, it was certainly after the First Jewish War and probably lingered after the Second (132–35 CE). Rather than seeing a sharp and immediate divide, it is better to see a gradual distinction between the two groups, especially after these wars and as the Jesus-movement became more Gentile centered (e.g., Acts 13–28).

20. Whether or not their experiences were unusual is a matter of debate since women's stories are rarely told in the ancient world, and even more rarely told from their perspectives (compare Dinah in Genesis 34). The women in Matt 1:1–17 have sex outside of

culturally expected marriages, but each is also the victim of patriarchal societies seeking to regulate her sexuality. Their maneuvering highlights their ingenuity and, as the biblical tradition relates, their righteousness.

21. Beverly Roberts Gaventa, *Mary: Glimpses of the Mother of Jesus*, SNTP (Columbia: University of South Carolina Press, 1995), 41.

22. See the discussion of anti-Judaism in the Christian Apocrypha in Chapter 7 and Amy-Jill Levine, "Matthew, Mark, and Luke: Good News or Bad?," in *Jesus, Judaism, and Christian Anti-Judaism: Reading the New Testament after the Holocaust*, ed. Paula Fredriksen and Adele Reinhartz (Louisville: Westminster John Knox, 2002), 87–92.

23. Raimo Hakola provides a helpful overview of social identity theory in *Reconsidering Johannine Christianity: A Social Identity Approach*, BW (London: Routledge, 2015), 24–29.

24. Rodney Reeves, "The Gospel of Matthew," in *The State of New Testament Studies: A Survey of Recent Research*, ed. Scot McKnight and Nijay K. Gupta (Grand Rapids, MI: Baker Academic, 2019), 290–93.

Chapter 4

1. The language of "disability" can be construed negatively, but that is not my intention here. I am using this word because of its connection to the larger field of disability studies, which is a growing area of interest for biblical scholars. Sarah J. Melcher, Mikeal C. Parsons, and Amos Yong, eds., *The Bible and Disability: A Commentary*, SRTD (Waco, TX: Baylor University Press, 2017).

2. "God-fearers" were Gentiles who worshiped the God of Israel but were not full Jewish converts, usually because they, or the male head of their household, did not undergo circumcision.

3. John T. Carroll, *Luke: A Commentary*, NTL (Louisville: Westminster John Knox, 2012), 21–22.

4. Mikeal C. Parsons, *Luke: Storyteller, Interpreter, Evangelist* (Peabody, MA: Hendrickson, 2007), 1–11.

5. Parsons, *Luke*, 40–47.

6. Carroll, *Luke*, 5–6.

7. Colleen Conway supplies an excellent overview of Roman-era masculinity in her book *Behold the Man: Jesus and Greco-Roman Masculinity* (Oxford: Oxford University Press, 2008), 15–34. Not all people are born biologically male or female; this was also true in the Roman world. Rather than genitalia, ancients focused on performance as revealing true gender, either masculine or feminine. Anything less than perfect masculinity was considered feminine to some degree. Rather than a binary, it is better to see gender as a spectrum.

8. Mikeal C. Parsons, *Body and Character in Luke and Acts: The Subversion of Physiognomy in Early Christianity*, 2nd ed. (Waco, TX: Baylor University Press, 2011), 17–65; Karl Allen Kuhn, *The Kingdom according to Luke and Acts: A Social, Literary, and Theological Introduction* (Grand Rapids, MI: Baker Academic, 2014), 3–22; Brittany E. Wilson, *Unmanly Men: Refigurations of Masculinity in Luke-Acts* (Oxford: Oxford University Press, 2015), 39–75.

9. I am using the term "traits" since it makes more sense for contemporary readers. Greco-Roman writers used the term *topoi*, which means "places." They had extensive lists of "places" that made up a person, or what we would call personality (see Chapter 1 and Chapter 5).

10. Suetonius, *Jul.* 45.2. Emperors wore wigs to hide thinning hair and to influence and reflect popular hairstyles (*Dom.* 18; *Otho* 12.1).

11. Emperors also acted as mediators between gods and humanity. Augustus began the legend of divine lineage in Rome, but the idea of divine election was not new to the ancient Mediterranean world. The implication of these stories is that challenging rulers is equal to challenging the gods. Conway, *Behold the Man*, 35–49.

12. Kuhn, *Kingdom*, 10–11.

13. Turid Karlsen Seim, *The Double Message: Patterns of Gender in Luke and Acts* (Nashville: Abingdon, 1994); Jennifer A. Glancy, *Slavery as Moral Problem in the Early Church and Today*, Facets (Minneapolis: Fortress, 2011).

14. Zeus was the "god of hospitality" (Zeus Xenios) and often traveled in disguise as a "stranger" (*xenios*) to test humans. He blessed those who showed hospitality (*xenia*) and punished those who didn't

(e.g., Ovid, *Metam.* 1.212–44; 8.626–724). For more examples see Andrew E. Arterbury, *Entertaining Angels: Early Christian Hospitality in Its Mediterranean Setting*, NTM 8 (Sheffield: Sheffield Phoenix, 2005), 15–54.

15. This short retelling of Abraham's story is not to suggest he is perfect. Indeed, his own experience being a stranger in the land makes God's instructions for him to expel Hagar and his son, Ishmael, into the wilderness even more shocking (Gen 21:10–14). In the story, God intervenes to help Hagar and Ishmael in the wilderness (21:15–20).

16. Several of Luke's unique stories are elaborately developed, such as the comparison between Zechariah and Mary at the beginning or Jesus's meeting the disciples on the way to Emmaus in Luke 24. When Luke has the freedom to craft his own version of events, his artistic and rhetorical abilities are pronounced. On Luke's use of rhetoric: Parsons, *Luke as Storyteller*, 17–32; Keith A. Reich, *Figuring Jesus: The Power of Rhetorical Figures of Speech in the Gospel of Luke*, BIS 107 (Leiden: Brill, 2011).

17. For more nuanced readings of Jesus's parables see Amy-Jill Levine, *Short Stories by Jesus: The Enigmatic Parables of a Controversial Rabbi* (New York: HarperOne, 2014).

18. Aristotle, *Rhet.* 1.9.38–41; Cicero, *Top.* 3.11; Theon, *Prog.* 108–9; Quintilian, *Inst.* 5.10–11.

19. On Jewish constructions of wives as houses see Alicia D. Myers, *Blessed among Women? Mothers and Motherhood in the New Testament* (Oxford: Oxford University Press, 2017), 31–38. Greco-Roman writings more often construe women's wombs as jars.

20. For more on Zechariah's muting see Wilson, *Unmanly Men*, 90–112.

21. Beverly Roberts Gaventa, *Mary: Glimpses of the Mother of Jesus*, SNTP (Minneapolis: Fortress, 1999), 54. On a spirit's (breath, air, *pneuma*) role in conception see Myers, *Blessed among Women*, 44–51, 59–69.

22. This woman is commonly mistaken as Mary Magdalene, but she is unnamed in Luke's account and identified as Mary of Bethany in John 12:1–8. For a history of interpretation see Jaime Clark-Soles, *The New Testament and the Christian Believer* (Louisville: Westminster John Knox, 2008), 36–42.

23. The Greek word *dikaiosyne* in Luke 23:47 means both "innocent" (NRSV) and "righteous."

Chapter 5

1. Beverly Roberts Gaventa, *Acts*, ANTC (Nashville: Abingdon, 2003), 175, rightly notes the disciples are not *commanded* to witness but are *promised* they will do so. The Greek verb is not an imperative, but a future indicative, which indicates a future reality.
2. Acts 1:8 indicates *where* disciples witness, rather than the origins of those to whom they witness. For example, Phillip preaches to an Ethiopian official in 8:26–40 while he is in Judea. Even though the Ethiopian returns home afterward, Acts focuses on the missionary activity performed *in* Judea regardless of where it continues beyond that point. Acts does not claim to be the whole story of all Jesus's disciples.
3. For a recent overview see Craig S. Keener, *Acts*, NCBC (Cambridge: Cambridge University Press, 2020), 46–52.
4. Ancient historians regularly avoided first-person narration, even for events in which they participated A. J. M. Wedderburn, "The 'We'-Passages in Acts: On the Horns of a Dilemma," *ZNW* 93 (2002): 78–98, provides a succinct overview of the debate.
5. Gaventa, *Acts*, 27.
6. This genre also explains why Acts ends as abruptly as it does. Paul's death is not narrated because his arrival in Rome fulfills Jesus's mission for him (19:21, 23:11). The story, however, is no more about Paul than it is about any other apostle; it is about the witnessing activity of disciples filled with the Holy Spirit. The book of Acts cannot have a tight ending because this activity continues and will continue, in Acts' perspective, until Jesus returns (1:10–11).
7. Lucian, *How to Write History*, 49–55; see also John Marincola, ed., *A Companion to Greek and Roman Historiography*, BCAW (Malden, MA: Blackwell, 2007).
8. *Hist.*, 1.22.1; C. F. Smith, trans., *Thucydides: A History of the Peloponnesian War*, 4 vols., LCL (Cambridge, MA: Harvard University Press, 1919–23).

9. A few scholars argue for a later date based on differences between Luke and Acts. Although written by the same author, Acts was finished twenty to thirty years later, they suggest, around 125 CE. Mikeal C. Parsons and Richard I. Pervo, *Rethinking the Unity of Luke and Acts* (Minneapolis: Fortress, 2007); Andrew F. Gregory and C. Kavin Rowe, eds., *Rethinking the Unity and Reception of Luke and Acts* (Columbia: South Carolina University Press, 2010).

10. The *Acts of Peter* and *Acts of Paul* describe their martyrdoms under Nero, around 64 CE. See Chapter 7.

11. Theon, *Prog.* 78.

12. Pseudo-Aristotle, *Rhet. Alex.* 29.31–34; Quintilian, *Inst.* 12.6.1–7, 12.11.1–8.

13. Gregory E. Sterling, "Turning to God: Conversion in Greek-Speaking Judaism and Early Christianity," in *Scripture and Traditions: Essays on Early Judaism and Christianity in Honor of Carl R. Holladay*, ed. Patrick Gray and Gail R. O'Day, NovTSup 129 (Leiden: Brill, 2008), 73. Sterling provides an excellent overview of all these categories as well as the language used in these works.

14. Such as Aseneth's fateful encounter with the handsome Joseph, or Protagoras's witnessing the philosopher Democritus's brilliance (*Jos. Asen.* 5–9; Aulus Gellius, *Noct. att.* 5.3.1).

15. *Jos. Asen.* 1, 8–9, 14–17, 23–29. Some other examples: Protagoras was already clever (Aulus Gellius, *Noct. att.* 5.3.1–7); Plutarch's Cilician ruler was already seeking truth (*Mor.* 434.d–f); even stories of Abraham's conversion describe his disgust with religious practices around him before he is confronted by God (*Apoc. Ab.* 8.1–6).

16. E.g., Helen Barrett Montgomery, *The Bible and Missions* (West Medford, MA: Central Committee on the Study of Foreign Missions, 1920), 83.

17. Repent (*metano-*): 2:38, 3:19, 5:31, 8:22, 11:18, 13:24, 17:30, 19:4, 20:21, 26:20; "turn from" (*epistreph-*) 3:19, 9:35, 11:21, 14:15, 15:19, 36, 16:18, 26:18, 20, 28:27. For more on this language, see Sterling, "Turning to God."

18. Gaventa, *Acts*, 54–56.

19. Bruce W. Longenecker, *Rhetoric at the Boundaries: The Art and Theology of the New Testament* (Waco, TX: Baylor University Press, 2005), esp. 165–252.

20. Gaventa, *Acts*, 320; Troy Troftgruben, *A Conclusion Unhindered: A Study of the Ending of Acts within Its Literary Environment*, WUNT 2/28 (Tübingen: Mohr Siebeck, 2010).

21. Gaventa, *Acts*, 74–75; Mikeal C. Parsons, *Acts*, PCNT (Grand Rapids, MI: Baker Academic, 2008), 37; Keener, *Acts*, 123–24.

22. Virgil, *Aen.* 2.679–91. See also Livy, 1.39; Pliny, *Nat.* 2.37.

23. For more see Alicia D. Myers, "Dreams, Visions, and Prophecies," *Christian Reflection* (May 2015): 21–27. Available online: https://www.baylor.edu/content/services/document.php/244020.pdf.

24. For a more thorough analysis see Brittany E. Wilson, *Unmanly Men: Refigurations of Masculinity in Luke-Acts* (Oxford: Oxford University Press, 2015), 113–49.

25. Acts 8:37 is a later insertion.

Chapter 6

1. Eve-Marie Becker, Helen K. Bond, and Catrin H. Williams, eds., *John's Transformation of Mark* (London: T&T Clark, 2021).

2. See especially Kasper Bro Larsen, *Recognizing the Stranger: Recognition Scenes in the Gospel of John*, BIS 93 (Leiden: Brill, 2008).

3. Pliny the Younger, *Epistulae ad Trajanum*.

4. R. Alan Culpepper, *John the Son of Zebedee: The Life of a Legend*, SNTP (Minneapolis: Fortress, 2000), esp. 56–88.

5. J. Louis Martyn, *History and Theology of the Fourth Gospel*, rev. ed., NTL (Louisville: Westminster John Knox, 2003); Raymond E. Brown, *Community of the Beloved Disciple: The Life, Love, and Hates of an Individual Church in New Testament Times* (Mahwah, NJ: Paulist Press, 1979).

6. Adele Reinhartz, *Cast Out of the Covenant: Jews and Anti-Judaism in the Gospel of John* (Lanham, MD: Lexington / Fortress Academic, 2018), esp. 116–25.

7. Reinhartz (*Cast Out of the Covenant*, 161–62) argues the Gospel creates its own community, while earlier scholars follow Richard

Bauckham's lead and suggest a general audience of all Christians for the Gospel (Bauckham, *The Testimony of the Beloved Disciple* [Grand Rapids, MI: Baker Academic, 2007], 113–23; Edward W. Klink III, *The Sheep of the Fold: The Audience and Origin of the Gospel of John*, SNTSMS 141 [Cambridge: Cambridge University Press, 2007], 249–50). Mary Coloe likewise differs from the majority by arguing for an original audience made up of both Gentiles and Jews ("Gentiles in the Gospel of John: Narrative Possibilities—John 12:12–43," in *Attitudes to Gentiles in Ancient Judaism and Early Christianity*, ed. David C. Sim and James S. McLaren, LNTS 499 [London: Bloomsbury / T&T Clark, 2013], 222–23).

8. Warren Carter, *John and Empire: Initial Explorations* (London: T&T Clark, 2008), 69–72.

9. Larsen, *Recognizing the Stranger*, 25–28.

10. For more on these philosophies see David Sedley, ed., *The Cambridge Companion to Greek and Roman Philosophy* (Cambridge: Cambridge University Press, 2003).

11. The serenity prayer is usually credited to Reinhold Niebuhr, although its roots could stretch back further. Fred R. Shapiro, "Who Wrote the Serenity Prayer," *Yale Alumni Magazine*, July–August 2008.

12. Shaye J. D. Cohen, *From the Maccabees to the Mishnah*, 3rd ed. (Louisville: Westminster John Knox, 2014), 47–50.

13. Larsen, *Recognizing the Stranger*, 29; Aristotle, *Poet.* 16 (1454b18–1455a12).

14. George L. Parsenios ("Defining and Debating Divine Identity in Mark and John," in Becker, Bond, and Williams, *John's Transformation of Mark*, 72–74) discusses the uses of "being" (*eimi*) and "becoming" (*ginomai*) throughout John to illustrate this point. The Word has eternality; it "was" from the beginning (1:1–5). When the Word "becomes" flesh as Jesus, however, he also participates in the temporal existence of humanity (1:14–17).

15. For example, Peder Borgen, *The Gospel of John: More Light from Philo, Paul and Archaeology: The Scriptures, Tradition, Settings, Meaning*, NovTSup 154 (Leiden: Brill, 2014), 43–66.

16. C. H. Dodd, *The Interpretation of the Fourth Gospel* (Cambridge: Cambridge University Press, 1953), stresses

connections to Plato and Philo (pp. 139–40); Troels Engberg-Pederson, *John and Philosophy: A New Reading of the Fourth Gospel* (Oxford: Oxford University Press, 2017), stresses Stoic connections.

17. See the recent conversation in R. Alan Culpepper and Paul N. Anderson, eds., *John and Judaism: A Contested Relationship in Context*, RBS 87 (Atlanta: SBL Press, 2017).

18. There is some debate on the tense of "believing" in 20:31, but most scholars argue the Gospel is written to people who already believe even if it could also be used for evangelistic purposes. See Jo-Ann A. Brant, *John*, PCNT (Grand Rapids, MI: Baker Academic, 2011), 274.

19. On Jesus's parables in John see Ruben Zimmermann, *Puzzling the Parables: Methods and Interpretation* (Minneapolis: Fortress, 2015), 333–39.

20. John's Gospel presents Jesus's ministry lasting three years. The Synoptics only record one Passover and, thus, imply Jesus's ministry lasted a year.

21. For helpful background see Catrin H. Williams, *I Am He: The Interpretations of "Anî Hû" in Jewish and Early Christian Literature*, WUNT 2/113 (Tübingen: Mohr Siebeck, 2000).

22. Most earlier readers also interpreted John the Baptist's witness to include 1:15–18, instead of stopping at verse 16. While I find the extension of John's words persuasive, I will represent the consensus view here (Brant, *John*, 35–37; Alicia D. Myers, *Reading John and 1, 2, 3 John*, RNT 2nd Series [Macon, GA: Smyth & Helwys, 2019], 43–44).

23. For a more in-depth discussion of this history see Myers, *Reading John*, 37–43.

24. R. Alan Culpepper, "The Pivot of John's Prologue," *NTS* 27 (1980): 1–31.

25. Jo-Ann A. Brant, *Dialogue and Drama: Elements of Greek Tragedy in the Fourth Gospel* (Peabody, MA: Hendrickson, 2004), 17–26.

26. Alicia D. Myers, *Blessed among Women? Mothers and Motherhood in the New Testament* (Oxford: Oxford University Press, 2017), 48–51, 68–69.

27. For a more complete version of this argument see Alicia D. Myers, "'Jesus Said to Them': The Adaptation of Juridical Rhetoric in John 5:19–47," *JBL* 132 (2013): 415–30.

Chapter 7

1. For a helpful overview of the history and creation of the Christian Apocrypha see Annette Yoshiko Reed, "The Afterlives of New Testament Apocrypha," *JBL* 133 (2015): 401–25.
2. Kasper Bro Larsen, "Fan Fiction and Early Christian Apocrypha," *ST* 73 (2019): 43–59. See also ReligionForBreakfast, "Star Wars Fan Fiction Explains Early Christian Apocrypha," *YouTube*, available online: https://www.youtube.com/watch?v=rTTRIA_YWIA, accessed 2 November 2020.
3. A "canon" is a closed list of books considered authoritative for a given community. The word "canon" (*kanon*) means "measure" or "standard." Canonical approaches are helpful for showing us how reading the Christian Bible as canon has influenced interpretations and history of traditions. It can also be a way of understanding the larger "Christian story" in presentations of what is often called "narrative theology" (e.g., Andrew E. Arterbury, W. H. Bellinger Jr., and Derek S. Dodson, *Engaging the Christian Scriptures: An Introduction to the Bible*, 2nd ed. [Grand Rapids, MI: Baker Academic, 2021]). Macro- and micro-readings of the Christian Bible should happen in conversation with one another.
4. Bruce M. Metzger, *The Canon of the New Testament: Its Origin, Development and Significance* (Oxford: Oxford University Press, 1997); James A. Sanders and Lee M. McDonald, eds., *The Canon Debate* (Grand Rapids, MI: Baker Academic, 2002). For a brief overview see Warren Carter, *Seven Events That Shaped the New Testament World* (Louisville: Westminster John Knox, 2013), 133–54.
5. Scholars developed collections of these writings and published them together, implying an association between these writings that did not exist when they were first composed. Nevertheless, these collections make accessing these works convenient for contemporary readers. Bart D. Ehrman, trans., *The Apostolic Fathers*,

2 vols., LCL (Cambridge, MA: Harvard University Press, 2003). Church fathers (or "patristics") are often categorized as "ante-Nicene fathers" and "post-Nicene Fathers," relating them to the first ecumenical creed of Christianity, the Nicene Creed of 325 CE.

6. See Chapter 1 on understanding ideas of authorship in the ancient world primarily as authorization and authority.

7. See the discussion of Judaism in Chapter 3.

8. Athanasius lists the four canonical Gospels and Acts first, followed by the seven catholic letters, and then the Letters of Paul, also in different order and including the Letter to the Hebrews. The list ends with the Revelation of John.

9. Reed, "Afterlives," 408–9. Athanasius and others called "apocryphal" the writings that scholars later defined as "Old Testament Pseudepigrapha." Reed argues it was not until the invention of the printing press that scholars grouped Christian apocryphal writings together as a type of countercanon (411). She suggests this distinction led scholars largely to abandon the study of these works until a recent resurgence of interest.

10. Larsen, "Fan Fiction," 50–53.

11. Tony Burke, *Secret Scriptures Revealed: A New Introduction to the Christian Apocrypha* (Grand Rapids, MI: Eerdmans, 2013), 24–43.

12. My division is loosely based on those of J. K. Elliott, *The Apocryphal New Testament: A Collection of Apocryphal Christian Literature in an English Translation Based on M. R. James* (Oxford: Oxford University Press, 2009) and Bart D. Ehrman and Zlatko Pleše, eds. and trans., *The Other Gospels: Accounts of Jesus from outside the New Testament* (Oxford: Oxford University Press, 2014). Fred Lapham, *An Introduction to the New Testament Apocrypha*, UBW (London: T&T Clark, 2003), arranges his discussion based on places of origin for the writings.

13. For more on ancient traditions about Jesus as a child see Stephen J. Davis, *Christ Child: Cultural Memories of a Young Jesus* (New Haven, CT: Yale University Press, 2014).

14. Translations are from Elliott, *Apocryphal New Testament*, unless otherwise noted.

15. Elliott, *Apocryphal New Testament*, 133–35, provides a chart connecting sayings from *Gos. Thom.* to sayings in the canonical Gospels.

16. April D. DeConick, *The Gnostic New Age: How a Countercultural Spirituality Revolutionized Religion from Antiquity to Today* (New York: Columbia University Press, 2016), 1–18.

17. Colleen M. Conway, *Behold the Man: Jesus and Greco-Roman Masculinity* (Oxford: Oxford University Press, 2008), 15–34.

18. The Pilate Cycle includes *The Gospel of Nicodemus* (also called *The Acts of Pilate*), *Christ's Descent into Hell*, various letters supposedly from Pilate, *The Death of Pilate*, *The Narrative of Joseph of Arimathea*, and more. Although the completed collection dates from the fifth century, elements could be much earlier. These traditions continued to be developed well into the Middle Ages (Elliott, *Apocryphal New Testament*, 164–66; Burke, *Secret Scriptures*, 80–84).

19. While the traditional reading interprets the cross speaking, Mark Goodacre suggests the text makes better sense if it refers to Jesus speaking as the "one crucified one." See Mark Goodacre, "A Walking, Talking Cross or the Walking, Talking Crucified One? A Conjectural Emendation in the Gospel of Peter," presented Society of Biblical Literature International Meeting (London, July 2011); Deane Galbraith, "Whence the Giant Jesus and His Talking Cross? The Resurrection in *Gospel of Peter* 10.39–42 as Prophetic Fulfillment of LXX Psalm 18," *JSNT* 63 (2017): 473–91.

20. Elaine Pagels, *The Gnostic Gospels*, rev. ed. (New York: Vintage Books, 1989).

21. Karen L. King, *The Gospel of Mary Magdala: Jesus and the First Woman Apostle* (Santa Rosa, CA: Polebridge Press, 2003). See also the discussion of Marys in the NT in *Which Mary? The Marys of Early Christian Tradition*, ed. F. Stanley Jones, SBLSymS 19 (Leiden: Brill, 2002). Although most scholars believe Mary Magdalene is the Mary of this gospel, others have suggested it is Jesus's mother or some sort of blended tradition of Marys (Stephen Shoemaker, "A Case of Mistaken Identity? Naming the Gnostic Mary," in Jones, *Which Mary*, 5–30).

22. Elliott, *Apocryphal New Testament*, 229–511; Bart D. Ehrman, *Lost Scriptures: Books That Did Not Make It into the New Testament* (Oxford: Oxford University Press, 2003), 91–154; Jeremy W. Barrier, *The Acts of Paul and Thecla: A Critical Introduction*

and Commentary, WUNT 2/270 (Tübingen: Mohr Siebeck, 2009), 23–24.

23. Andrew S. Jacobs, "'Her Own Proper Kinship': Marriage, Class and Women in the Apocryphal Acts of the Apostles," in *A Feminist Companion to the New Testament Apocrypha*, ed. Amy-Jill Levine with Maria Mayo Robbins (Cleveland: Pilgrim, 2006), 18–19.

24. For more on this see the essays in Levine, *Feminist Companion*, especially, Cornelia B. Horn, "Suffering Children, Parental Authority and the Quest for Liberation? A Tale of Three Girls in the *Acts of Paul (and Thecla)*, the *Act(s) of Peter*, the *Acts of Nereus and Achilleus*, and the *Epistle of Pseudo-Titus*," 121–30.

25. Recorded in the Coptic *Act of Peter*. See "Peter's Daughter," in Elliott, *Apocryphal New Testament*, 397–98.

26. For more on Thecla's popularity see Stephen J. Davis, *The Cult of St Thecla: A Tradition of Women's Piety in Late Antiquity*, ECS (Oxford: Oxford University Press, 2001).

27. Many denominations have supplemental writings explaining practice or doctrine. Reformed traditions value works of John Calvin, while Lutherans prize Martin Luther's writings. United Methodists have a *Book of Discipline* and Roman Catholics have a variety of papal encyclicals. Even nondenominational Protestants have authoritative voices they value over others. See Jaime Clark-Soles, *The New Testament and the Christian Believer* (Louisville: Westminster John Knox, 2008), 1–12, 127–48, for an insightful discussion.

Chapter 8

1. Charles H. Talbert, ed., *Reimarus: Fragments*, trans. Ralph S. Fraser (New York: SCM Press, 1970; repr. Eugene, OR: Wipf & Stock, 2009), esp. 27–43. For helpful overviews of historical Jesus research see Dale C. Allison Jr., *The Historical Christ and the Theological Jesus* (Grand Rapids, MI: Eerdmans, 2009), 1–30; Jaime Clark-Soles, *Engaging the Word: The New Testament and the Christian Believer* (Louisville: Westminster John Knox, 2008), 103–26; Chris Keith and Anthony LeDonne, eds., *Jesus, Criteria, and the Demise of Authenticity* (London: T&T Clark, 2012).

2. Ernst Käsemann, "The Problem of the Historical Jesus," in *Essays on New Testament Themes*, trans. W. J. Montague (Philadelphia: Fortress, 1982), 15–47.

3. Albert Schweitzer, *The Quest of the Historical Jesus: A Critical Study of Its Progress from Reimarus to Wrede*, trans. W. Montgomery (New York: Macmillan, 1968), 309–12.

4. The following is taken from Allison, *Historical Christ*. For a more complete overview of his argument see Dale C. Allison Jr., *Constructing Jesus: Memory, Imagination, and History* (Grand Rapids, MI: Baker Academic, 2010).

5. Allison, *Historical Christ*, 28.

6. Allison, *Historical Christ*, 53–78.

7. Allison, *Historical Christ*, 80–103.

BIBLIOGRAPHY

Allison, Dale C., Jr. *Constructing Jesus: Memory, Imagination, and History*. Grand Rapids, MI: Baker Academic, 2010.

Allison, Dale C., Jr. *The Historical Christ and the Theological Jesus*. Grand Rapids, MI: Eerdmans, 2009.

Anderson, Paul N. "The Community That Raymond Brown Left Behind: Reflections on the Johannine Dialectical Situation." Pages 47–94 in *Communities in Dispute: Current Scholarship on the Johannine Epistles*. Edited by Alan R. Culpepper and Paul N. Anderson. ECL 13. Atlanta: SBL Press, 2014.

Anderson, Paul N. *The Riddles of the Fourth Gospel: An Introduction to John*. Minneapolis: Fortress, 2011.

Anderson, Paul N., Felix Just, and Tom Thatcher, eds. *John, Jesus, and History*. Vol. 1: *Critical Appraisals of Critical Views*. SBLSymS 44. Atlanta: SBL Press, 2007.

Arterbury, Andrew E. *Entertaining Angels: Early Christian Hospitality in Its Mediterranean Setting*. NTM 8. Sheffield: Sheffield Phoenix, 2005.

Arterbury, Andrew E., W. H. Bellinger Jr., and Derek S. Dodson. *Engaging the Christian Scriptures: An Introduction to the Bible*. 2nd ed. Grand Rapids, MI: Baker Academic, 2021.

Barrier, Jeremy W. *The Acts of Paul and Thecla: A Critical Introduction and Commentary*. WUNT 2/270. Tübingen: Mohr Siebeck, 2009.

Bauckham, Richard. "About People, by People, for People: Gospel Genre and Audiences." Pages 113–45 in *The Gospels for All Christians: Rethinking the Gospel Audiences*. Edited by Richard Bauckham. Grand Rapids, MI: Eerdmans, 1998.

Bauckham, Richard. "For Whom Were the Gospels Written?" Pages 9–48 in *The Gospels for All Christians: Rethinking the Gospel Audiences*. Edited by Richard Bauckham. Grand Rapids, MI: Eerdmans, 1998.

Bauckham, Richard. *The Testimony of the Beloved Disciple*. Grand Rapids, MI: Baker Academic, 2007.

Becker, Eve-Marie, Helen K. Bond, and Catrin H. Williams, eds. *John's Transformation of Mark*. London: T&T Clark, 2021.

Boomershine, Tom. "Tom Boomershine Performs Mark's Gospel." *YouTube*. https://www.youtube.com/playlist?list=PL7DR0ecPG8I1WonZetQ6-Fj7gC4g4ED-L. Accessed 4 September 2020.

Borgen, Peder. *The Gospel of John: More Light from Philo, Paul and Archaeology: The Scriptures, Tradition, Settings, Meaning*. NovTSup 154. Leiden: Brill, 2014.

Brant, Jo-Ann A. *Dialogue and Drama: Elements of Greek Tragedy in the Fourth Gospel*. Peabody, MA: Hendrickson, 2004.

Brant, Jo-Ann A. *John*. PCNT. Grand Rapids, MI: Baker Academic, 2011.

Brown, Raymond E. *Community of the Beloved Disciple: The Life, Love, and Hates of an Individual Church in New Testament Times*. Mahwah, NJ: Paulist Press, 1979.

Burke, Tony. *Secret Scriptures Revealed: A New Introduction to the Christian Apocrypha*. Grand Rapids, MI: Eerdmans, 2013.

Burridge, Richard A. *What Are the Gospels? A Comparison with Greco-Roman Biography*. 2nd ed. Grand Rapids, MI: Eerdmans, 2004.

Carroll, John T. *Luke: A Commentary*. NTL. Louisville: Westminster John Knox, 2012.

Carter, Warren. *John and Empire: Initial Explorations*. London: T&T Clark, 2008.

Carter, Warren. *Seven Events That Shaped the New Testament World*. Louisville: Westminster John Knox, 2013.

Clark-Soles, Jaime. *Engaging the Word: The New Testament and the Christian Believer*. Louisville: Westminster John Knox, 2008.

Cohen, Shaye J. D. *From the Maccabees to the Mishnah*. 3rd ed. Louisville: Westminster John Knox, 2014.

Collins, John J. *The Apocalyptic Imagination: An Introduction to Jewish Apocalyptic Literature*. 2nd ed. BRS. Grand Rapids, MI: Eerdmans, 1998.

Coloe, Mary. "Gentiles in the Gospel of John: Narrative Possibilities— John 12:12–43." Pages 209–23 in *Attitudes to Gentiles in Ancient Judaism and Early Christianity*. Edited by David C. Sim and James S. McLaren. LNTS 499. London: Bloomsbury / T&T Clark, 2013.

Conway, Colleen M. *Behold the Man: Jesus and Greco-Roman Masculinity*. Oxford: Oxford University Press, 2008.

Corbeill, Anthony. "Education in the Roman Republic: Creating Traditions." Pages 261–87 in *Education in Greek and Roman Antiquity*. Edited by Yun Lee Too. Leiden: Brill, 2001.

Covington, Dennis. *Salvation on Sand Mountain: Snake Handling and Redemption in Southern Appalachia*. Philadelphia: Da Capo Press, 2009.

Culpepper, R. Alan. *John the Son of Zebedee: The Life of a Legend*. SNTP. Minneapolis: Fortress, 2000.

Culpepper, R. Alan. "The Pivot of John's Prologue." *NTS* 27 (1980): 1–31.

Culpepper, R. Alan, and Paul N. Anderson, eds. *John and Judaism: A Contested Relationship in Context*. RBS 87. Atlanta: SBL Press, 2017.

Davis, Stephen J. *Christ Child: Cultural Memories of a Young Jesus*. New Haven, CT: Yale University Press, 2014.

Davis, Stephen J. *The Cult of St Thecla: A Tradition of Women's Piety in Late Antiquity*. ECS. Oxford: Oxford University Press, 2001.

DeConick, April D. *The Gnostic New Age: How a Countercultural Spirituality Revolutionized Religion from Antiquity to Today*. New York: Columbia University Press, 2016.

Dodd, C. H. *The Interpretation of the Fourth Gospel*. Cambridge: Cambridge University Press, 1953.

Dowd, Sharyn. *Reading Mark: A Literary and Theological Commentary on the Second Gospel*. RNT. Macon, GA: Smyth & Helwys, 2000.

Dunn, James D. G. "The Gospel and the Gospels." *EQ* 85 (2013): 291–93.

Ehrman, Bart D., trans. *The Apostolic Fathers*. 2 vols. LCL. Cambridge, MA: Harvard University Press, 2003.

Ehrman, Bart D. *Lost Scriptures: Books That Did Not Make It into the New Testament*. Oxford: Oxford University Press, 2003.

Ehrman, Bart D., and Zlatko Pleše, eds. and trans. *The Other Gospels: Accounts of Jesus from outside the New Testament*. Oxford: Oxford University Press, 2014.

Elliott, J. K. *The Apocryphal New Testament: A Collection of Apocryphal Christian Literature in an English Translation Based on M. R. James*. Oxford: Oxford University Press, 2009.

Engberg-Pederson, Troels. *John and Philosophy: A New Reading of the Fourth Gospel*. Oxford: Oxford University Press, 2017.

Galbraith, Deane. "Whence the Giant Jesus and His Talking Cross? The Resurrection in *Gospel of Peter* 10.39–42 as Prophetic Fulfillment of LXX Psalm 18." *JSNT* 63 (2017): 473–91.

Gaventa, Beverly Roberts. *Acts*. ANTC. Nashville: Abingdon, 2003.

Gaventa, Beverly Roberts. *Mary: Glimpses of the Mother of Jesus*. SNTP. Columbia: University of South Carolina Press, 1995.

Gaventa, Beverly Roberts, and Patrick D. Miller, eds. *The Endings of Mark and the Ends of God: Essays in Memory of Donald Harrisville Juel*. Louisville: Westminster John Know, 2005.

Glancy, Jennifer A. *Slavery as Moral Problem in the Early Church and Today*. Facets. Minneapolis: Fortress, 2011.

Goodacre, Mark. *The Case against Q: Studies in Markan Priority and the Synoptic Problem*. Harrisburg, PA: Trinity Press International, 2002.

Goodacre, Mark. "A Walking, Talking Cross or the Walking, Talking Crucified One? A Conjectural Emendation in the Gospel of Peter." Presented at the Society of Biblical Literature International Meeting. London, July 2011.

Goulder, Michael. "Is Q a Juggernaut?" *JBL* 115 (1996): 667–81.

Gregory, Andrew F., and C. Kavin Rowe, eds. *Rethinking the Unity and Reception of Luke and Acts*. Columbia: South Carolina University Press, 2010.

Grubbs, Judith Evans, and Tim Parkin, eds. *The Oxford Handbook on Childhood and Education in the Classical World*. Oxford: Oxford University Press, 2013.

Hakola, Raimo. *Reconsidering Johannine Christianity: A Social Identity Approach*. BW. London: Routledge, 2015.

Horn, Cornelia B. "Suffering Children, Parental Authority and the Quest for Liberation? A Tale of Three Girls in the *Acts of Paul (and Thecla)*, the *Act(s) of Peter*, the *Acts of Nereus and Achilleus*, and the *Epistle of Pseudo-Titus*." Pages 121–30 in *A Feminist Companion to the New Testament Apocrypha*. Edited by Amy-Jill Levine with Maria Mayo Robbins. Cleveland: Pilgrim, 2006.

Jacobs, Andrew S. "'Her Own Proper Kinship': Marriage, Class and Women in the Apocryphal Acts of the Apostles." Pages 18–46 in *A Feminist Companion to the New Testament Apocrypha*. Edited by Amy-Jill Levine with Maria Mayo Robbins. Cleveland: Pilgrim, 2006.

Käsemann, Ernst. "The Problem of the Historical Jesus." Pages 15–47 in *Essays on New Testament Themes*. Translated by W. J. Montague. Philadelphia: Fortress, 1982.

Keener, Craig S. *Acts*. NCBC. Cambridge: Cambridge University Press, 2020.

Keener, Craig S. *Christobiography: Memory, History, and the Reliability of the Gospels*. Grand Rapids, MI: Eerdmans, 2019.

Keith, Chris. *The Gospel as Manuscript: An Early History of the Jesus Tradition as Material Artifact*. Oxford: Oxford University Press, 2020.

Keith, Chris, and Anthony LeDonne, eds. *Jesus, Criteria, and the Demise of Authenticity*. London: T&T Clark, 2012.

King, Karen L. *The Gospel of Mary Magdala: Jesus and the First Woman Apostle*. Santa Rosa, CA: Polebridge Press, 2003.

Kinlaw, Pamela E. *The Christ Is Jesus: Metamorphosis, Possession, and Johannine Christology*. SBLAB 18. Atlanta: SBL Press, 2005.

Kittel, G., and G. Friedrich, eds. *Theological Dictionary of the New Testament*. Translated by G. W. Bromiley. 10 vols. Grand Rapids, MI: Eerdmans, 1964–76.

Klink, Edward W., III. *The Sheep of the Fold: The Audience and Origin of the Gospel of John*. SNTSMS 141. Cambridge: Cambridge University, 2007.

Kuhn, Karl Allen. *The Kingdom according to Luke and Acts: A Social, Literary, and Theological Introduction*. Grand Rapids, MI: Baker Academic, 2014.

Lapham, Fred. *An Introduction to the New Testament Apocrypha*. UBW. London: T&T Clark, 2003.

Larsen, Kasper Bro. "Fan Fiction and Early Christian Apocrypha." *ST* 73 (2019): 43–59.

Larsen, Kasper Bro. *Recognizing the Stranger: Recognition Scenes in the Gospel of John*. BIS 93. Leiden: Brill, 2008.

Larsen, Matthew D. C. *Gospels before the Book*. Oxford: Oxford University Press, 2018.

Levine, Amy-Jill. "Matthew, Mark, and Luke: Good News or Bad?" Pages 77–98 in *Jesus, Judaism, and Christian Anti-Judaism: Reading the New Testament after the Holocaust*. Edited by Paula Fredriksen and Adele Reinhartz. Louisville: Westminster John Knox, 2002.

Levine, Amy-Jill. *Short Stories by Jesus: The Enigmatic Parables of a Controversial Rabbi*. New York: HarperOne, 2014.

Longenecker, Bruce W. *Rhetoric at the Boundaries: The Art and Theology of the New Testament*. Waco, TX: Baylor University Press, 2005.

Malbon, Elizabeth Struthers. *Hearing Mark: A Listener's Guide*. Harrisburg, PA: Trinity Press International, 2002.

Malbon, Elizabeth Struthers. *Mark's Jesus: Characterization as Narrative Christology*. Waco, TX: Baylor University Press, 2014.

Marcus, Joel. "Crucifixion as Parodic Exaltation." *JBL* 125 (2006): 111–25.

Marcus, Joel. *Mark 1–8*. AB 27. New York: Doubleday, 1999.

Marcus, Joel. *The Way of the Lord: Christological Exegesis of the Old Testament in the Gospel of Mark*. Louisville: Westminster John Knox, 1992.

Marincola, John, ed. *A Companion to Greek and Roman Historiography*. BCAW. Malden, MA: Blackwell, 2007.

Martínez, Florentino García, and Eibert J. C. Tigchelaar, eds. and trans. *The Dead Sea Scrolls: Study Edition*. 2 vols. Leiden: Brill; Grand Rapids, MA: Eerdmans, 1997.

Martyn, J. Louis. *History and Theology of the Fourth Gospel*. Rev. ed. NTL. Louisville: Westminster John Knox, 2003.

Melcher, Sarah J., Mikeal C. Parsons, and Amos Yong, eds. *The Bible and Disability: A Commentary*. SRTD. Waco, TX: Baylor University Press, 2017.

Metzger, Bruce M. *The Canon of the New Testament: Its Origin, Development and Significance*. Oxford: Oxford University Press, 1997.

Montgomery, Helen Barrett. *The Bible and Missions*. West Medford, MA: Central Committee on the Study of Foreign Missions, 1920.

Moss, Candida R. "Mark and Matthew." Pages 275–302 in *The Bible and Disability: A Commentary.* Edited by Sarah J. Melcher, Mikeal C. Parsons, and Amos Yong. Waco, TX: Baylor University Press, 2017.

Myers, Alicia D. *Blessed among Women? Mothers and Motherhood in the New Testament.* Oxford: Oxford University Press, 2017.

Myers, Alicia D. *Characterizing Jesus: A Rhetorical Analysis of the Fourth Gospel's Use of Scripture in Its Presentation of Jesus.* LNTS 458. London: Bloomsbury T&T Clark, 2012.

Myers, Alicia D. "Dreams, Visions, and Prophecies." *Christian Reflection* (May 2015): 21–27.

Myers, Alicia D. "'Jesus Said to Them': The Adaptation of Juridical Rhetoric in John 5:19–47." *JBL* 132 (2013): 415–30.

Myers, Alicia D. *Reading John and 1, 2, 3 John.* RNT 2nd Series. Macon, GA: Smyth & Helwys, 2019.

Myers, Alicia D., and Lindsey S. Jodrey. "Come and Read: Hermeneutics and Interpretive Perspectives in the Gospel of John." Pages 1–25 in *Come and Read: Interpretive Approaches to the Gospel of John.* IJL 1. Baltimore: Lexington / Fortress Academic, 2020.

Pagels, Elaine. *The Gnostic Gospels.* Rev. ed. New York: Vintage Books, 1989.

Parsenios, George L. "Defining and Debating Divine Identity in Mark and John." Pages 67–74 in *John's Transformation of Mark.* Edited by Eve-Marie Becker, Helen K. Bond, and Catrin H. Williams. London: T&T Clark, 2021.

Parsons, Mikeal C. *Acts.* PCNT. Grand Rapids, MI: Baker Academic, 2008.

Parsons, Mikeal C. *Body and Character in Luke and Acts: The Subversion of Physiognomy in Early Christianity.* 2nd ed. Waco, TX: Baylor University Press, 2011.

Parsons, Mikeal C. *Luke: Storyteller, Interpreter, Evangelist.* Peabody, MA: Hendrickson, 2007.

Parsons, Mikeal C., and Richard I. Pervo. *Rethinking the Unity of Luke and Acts.* Minneapolis: Fortress, 2007.

Pietersma, Albert, and Benjamin G. Wright, eds. *A New English Translation of the Septuagint.* Oxford: Oxford University Press, 2007.

Reed, Annette Yoshiko. "The Afterlives of New Testament Apocrypha." *JBL* 133 (2015): 401–25.

Reeves, Rodney. "The Gospel of Matthew." Pages 275–96 in *The State of New Testament Studies: A Survey of Recent Research*. Edited by Scot McKnight and Nijay K. Gupta. Grand Rapids, MI: Baker Academic, 2019.

Reich, Keith A. *Figuring Jesus: The Power of Rhetorical Figures of Speech in the Gospel of Luke*. BIS 107. Leiden: Brill, 2011.

Reinhartz, Adele. *Cast Out of the Covenant: Jews and Anti-Judaism in the Gospel of John*. Lanham, MD: Lexington / Fortress Academic, 2018.

ReligionForBreakfast. "Star Wars Fan Fiction Explains Early Christian Apocrypha." *YouTube*. https://www.youtube.com/watch?v=rTTRIA_YWIA. Accessed 2 November 2020.

Rhoads, David Joanna Dewey, and Donald Michie. *Mark as Story: An Introduction to the Narrative of a Gospel*. 3rd ed. Minneapolis: Fortress, 2012.

Sanders, James A., and Lee M. McDonald, eds. *The Canon Debate*. Grand Rapids, MI: Baker Academic, 2002.

Satlow, Michael L. "'Try to Be a Man': The Rabbinic Construction of Masculinity." *HTR* 89 (1996): 22–35.

Schweitzer, Albert. *The Quest of the Historical Jesus: A Critical Study of Its Progress from Reimarus to Wrede*. Translated by W. Montgomery. New York: Macmillan, 1968.

Sedley, David, ed. *The Cambridge Companion to Greek and Roman Philosophy*. Cambridge: Cambridge University Press, 2003.

Seim, Turid Karlsen. *The Double Message: Patterns of Gender in Luke and Acts*. Nashville: Abingdon, 1994.

Shapiro, Fred R. "Who Wrote the Serenity Prayer." *Yale Alumni Magazine*, July–August 2008.

Shoemaker, Stephen. "A Case of Mistaken Identity? Naming the Gnostic Mary." Pages 5–30 in *Which Mary? The Marys of Early Christian Tradition*. Edited by F. Stanley Jones. SBLSymS 19. Leiden: Brill, 2002.

Sim, David C. "The Gospel of Matthew and Galilee: An Evaluation of an Emerging Hypothesis." *ZNW* 107 (2016): 141–69.

Smith, C. F., trans. *Thucydides: A History of the Peloponnesian War*. 4 vols. LCL. Cambridge, MA: Harvard University Press, 1919–23.

Stadter, Philip. "Biography and History." Pages 528–32 in *A Companion to Greek and Roman Historiography*. Edited by John Marincola, BCAW. Malden, MA: Blackwell, 2008.

Stendahl, Krister. *The School of St. Matthew and Its Use of the Old Testament*. 2nd ed. Philadelphia: Fortress, 1968.

Sterling, Gregory E. "Turning to God: Conversion in Greek-Speaking Judaism and Early Christianity." Pages 69–95 in *Scripture and Traditions: Essays on Early Judaism and Christianity in Honor of Carl R. Holladay*. Edited by Patrick Gray and Gail R. O'Day. NovTSup 129. Leiden: Brill, 2008.

Talbert, Charles H., ed. *Reimarus: Fragments*. Translated by Ralph S. Fraser. New York: SCM Press, 1970. Repr. Eugene, OR: Wipf & Stock, 2009.

Talbert, Charles H. *What Is a Gospel?* Philadelphia: Fortress, 1977.

Thatcher, Tom. *Why John Wrote a Gospel: Jesus—Memory—History*. Louisville: Westminster John Knox, 2006.

Tolbert, Mary Ann. *Sowing the Gospel: Mark's World in Literary-Historical Perspective*. Minneapolis: Fortress, 1989.

Troftgruben, Troy. *A Conclusion Unhindered: A Study of the Ending of Acts within Its Literary Environment*. WUNT 2/28. Tübingen: Mohr Siebeck, 2010.

Ulrich, Daniel W. "The Missional Audience of the Gospel of Matthew." *CBQ* (2007): 64–83.

Walsh, Robyn Faith. *The Origins of Early Christian Literature: Contextualizing the New Testament within Greco-Roman Literary Culture*. Cambridge: Cambridge University Press, 2021.

Watts, Rikki E. *Isaiah's New Exodus in Mark*. BSL. Grand Rapids, MI: Baker Academic, 2001.

Wedderburn, A. J. M. "The 'We'-Passages in Acts: On the Horns of a Dilemma." *ZNW* 93 (2002): 78–98.

Williams, Catrin H. *I Am He: The Interpretations of "Anî Hû" in Jewish and Early Christian Literature*. WUNT 2/113. Tübingen: Mohr Siebeck, 2000.

Wilson, Brittany E. *Unmanly Men: Refigurations of Masculinity in Luke-Acts*. Oxford: Oxford University Press, 2015.

Zetterholm, Magnus. "The Jews of Antioch after the Fall of Jerusalem." *Bible Odyssey*, https://www.bibleodyssey.org/en/places/related-articles/jews-of-antioch-after-the-fall-of-jerusalem. Accessed 21 December 2020.

Zimmermann, Ruben. *Puzzling the Parables: Methods and Interpretation*. Minneapolis: Fortress, 2015.

INDEX

For the benefit of digital users, indexed terms that span two pages (e.g., 52–53) may, on occasion, appear on only one of those pages.

Tables and figures are indicated by *t* and *f* following the page number